Controlling 'Your
ANGER

7 Strategies to Master Emotions, Elevate Your Mindset and Take Ownership of Your Life

RONALD NORMANDY

UNCOVERING THE SIGNIFICANCE OF ANGER

Anger, often judged and suppressed, is a natural response to our challenges and injustices. It is rooted in our perspectives, shaped by cultural and societal factors, and influenced by our unique experiences. In these pages, we will journey through anger, exploring its multifaceted nature and unveiling the truths hidden beneath its stigma.

This book draws from a wealth of psychological research, real-life examples, and personal experiences to offer seven powerful strategies. These strategies will help you master your emotions and transcend the limitations that anger can impose. We will delve into the root causes of anger, unraveling its triggers and unveiling the transformative potential hidden within this potent emotion.

By understanding the purpose of anger and embracing healthy ways to express and manage it, you will unlock a world of personal growth and empowerment. Through these carefully curated strategies, you will learn to navigate your anger, channel its energy constructively, and gain mastery over your emotional responses. Each chapter presents practical exercises, insightful reflections, and actionable steps to empower you on your journey of self-discovery and emotional transformation.

This book is not merely about controlling anger; it is about transforming your mindset and taking ownership of your life. By honing your emotional intelligence and developing a growth-oriented mindset, you will gain the tools to navigate life's challenges with resilience and grace. As you begin this transformative journey, you will find that these strategies not only empower you in managing anger but also inspire personal growth in various aspects of your life.

Remember, change is a process that requires dedication and patience. It is in the commitment to our growth that we find the power to rewrite our stories and redefine our relationship with anger. Through the insights and wisdom shared within these pages, you will embark on a transformative journey toward emotional well-being, personal empowerment, and a life of purpose. Together, let us unveil the true potential of anger and harness its energy to create a life filled with authenticity, resilience, and inner peace.

With sincere support on your transformative journey,

Ronald Normandy

TABLE OF CONTENTS

YOUR INTRODUCTION TO ANGER

L et's take a moment to reflect on the importance of emotions in our lives. Emotions are not fleeting feelings; they are an essential part of who we are. They profoundly influence every aspect of our existence, shaping our thoughts, feelings, decisions, and actions. Each emotion has significance and power, crucial in maintaining our overall well-being. Like a well-coordinated orchestra, our emotions work together to create a beautiful symphony of life.

However, when the balance of our emotions is disrupted, we can feel overwhelmed and lose control. It is essential to recognize the distinct qualities of each emotion and understand how they contribute to our lives. Love brings warmth and compassion, fear protects us from harm, anger fuels our desire for justice, and joy gives us reasons to celebrate. Each emotion is unique and adds depth to our experiences, like different colors on a canvas.

Among all the emotions, anger is particularly complex and common. It can manifest in various ways, from explosive outbursts to subtle forms of expressing frustration. While there are times when anger is justified, it is crucial to find a balance in how we communicate it. Anger, like other emotions, is part of the rich tapestry of life, and experiencing a range of emotions makes us feel alive and conscious.

Emotions reflect the harmonious nature of a symphony, where each emotion plays a crucial role in creating a melody. Just as musical notes blend to produce a pleasing tune, our emotions work in concert to shape our experiences. Some emotions may take the spotlight, while others provide a supporting role, creating a balanced and beautiful composition. It is within our power to choose which emotions we allow to take center stage.

Consider anger as a powerful note in the orchestra of emotions. We can decide whether to let it rise and crescendo into an overwhelming display of fury and rage or to temper it, allowing it to subside gradually. We have a choice to make as we conduct our emotional symphony. It is essential to find the right balance, embracing and understanding our emotions fully.

By fully comprehending our emotions, we can harness their energy and use them as tools for personal growth and enriching our relationships. Just as a skilled conductor brings out the best in an orchestra, we can learn to channel our emotions in ways that enhance our lives and positively impact those around us. Through this mindful orchestration of our emotions, we can create a life filled with harmony, authenticity, and meaningful connections.

EMBRACING THE POTENTIAL OF ANGER

Anger is a primal and deeply rooted emotion that constantly challenges our ability to control it. Its presence can lead to destructive behaviors, harming our loved ones or unleashing frustrations upon strangers. However, the impact of anger reaches far beyond fleeting moments. It holds the potential to shape our physical and mental well-being profoundly. To overcome its destructive influence, we must confront anger head-on, acknowledging that it is more than a passing mood but a powerful energy that permeates our existence. By exploring its impact, understanding its essence, and harnessing it for constructive purposes, we can strive to master anger and break free from its harmful effects.

When we give in to anger, we risk losing our true selves and becoming unrecognizable. In those moments, we may unjustly lash out, say hurtful things, and harm those we deeply care about. The path anger takes us on is one of devastation, potentially leading to the loss of cherished relationships and everything we hold dear.

However, within its destructive potential, anger can also act as a catalyst for transformation. It possesses the power to ignite our determination, motivating us to stand up for our beliefs, fight for justice, and create positive change in the world. Anger can serve as the fuel that propels us toward self-improvement, inspiring us to strive for greatness and become resilient.

The effects of anger in our lives can become pervasive, impacting every aspect of our well-being. When left unchecked, anger can manifest as tension, anxiety, and physical ailments like headaches, muscle pain, and fatigue. Moreover, its influence extends to our mental health, contributing to feelings of depression, anxiety, and other psychological struggles. Despite the profound consequences, we often fall prey to anger's allure, allowing it to dominate and define us. However, we can take control of our anger, harnessing its potent energy and channeling it towards positive outcomes.

Rather than allowing anger to govern our actions, let us explore ways to channel it constructively. By doing so, we can propel ourselves forward, find motivation for personal growth, and positively contribute to the world around us. The ultimate impact of anger on our lives lies within our own hands. We have the choice to either let it destroy us or harness its transformative potential to inspire greatness within ourselves. By embracing and understanding our anger, we unlock a realm of possibilities and open ourselves up to a path of self discovery and growth.

The Impact of Personal Experiences

Personal experiences play a pivotal role in shaping the way individuals navigate and manage their anger. Our upbringing, the environmental conditions we experienced, and the relationships we have formed all contribute to our unique patterns of expressing and handling anger. For instance, individuals who grew up in households where shouting and aggression were commonplace may adopt anger as their primary mode of communication.

Lacking exposure to healthy emotional expression, they may resort to explosive outbursts when confronted with conflict. Conversely, individuals raised in environments where emotions were suppressed or disregarded may struggle to articulate their anger. The intensity of their feelings may make them uncomfortable, and they may find it challenging to assert themselves in situations that call for it.

People employ diverse strategies to manage their anger, reflecting their experiences and coping mechanisms. Some individuals resort to lashing out, using aggression to release their frustration. Others may adopt a passive aggressive approach, bottling their anger and expressing it indirectly. Unfortunately, in some cases, unresolved anger can be displaced onto unintended targets, leading to a cycle of harm. Some individuals may turn to substance abuse to escape reality and temporarily alleviate their anger. In contrast, others take proactive steps to address the root causes of their frustration and work toward resolution.

Furthermore, personal experiences influence how we perceive and respond to anger in others. If someone has been a victim of verbal or physical abuse, they may be more inclined to view anger as a potential threat, triggering defensive or aggressive responses. Our past encounters with anger also shape our beliefs about how individuals should handle expressing anger. Witnessing positive examples of effective anger management can inspire individuals to adopt similar strategies when confronted with their own emotions. By understanding how our personal experiences have shaped our relationship with anger, we can cultivate self-awareness and consciously choose how to express and manage our emotions.

The Unique Qualities of This Book

This book offers a unique perspective on the often overlooked issue of anger management. In a society where it is easy to dismiss and suppress our emotions, this book encourages us to confront and address our anger constructively. Unlike other resources that merely scratch the surface, this book delves deep into the roots of our anger, seeking to understand the complex interplay of emotions, experiences, and beliefs that contribute to our outbursts.

One of the key differentiators of this book is its emphasis on self-acceptance and self-understanding. Rather than solely focusing on managing anger symptoms, it guides readers on a transformative journey of acknowledging and accepting their flaws and imperfections. By delving into the underlying causes of anger and exploring our emotional landscapes, we can make lasting changes and become better versions of ourselves.

Another distinguishing feature of this book is its holistic approach to anger management. It goes beyond offering quick fixes or simple avoidance strategies. Instead, it recognizes that actual growth requires us to confront and navigate challenging situations with effective coping mechanisms. By empowering readers to recognize the signs and symptoms of anger, the book equips them with the tools needed to navigate unfavorable circumstances constructively and find effective resolutions.

Furthermore, this book extends its reach beyond individual readers. It emphasizes the importance of cultivating empathy and understanding, encouraging readers to not only manage their anger but also extend support to those around them who may be struggling with similar issues. By recognizing the signs of anger in others and providing constructive assistance, readers can foster a more compassionate and supportive community.

Ultimately, what makes this book truly unique is its commitment to personal growth and transformation. Recognizing that managing anger is a complex journey, the book acknowledges that it begins with small, incremental changes and the cultivation of new habits. By embarking on this path of self-discovery and continual improvement, readers are empowered to confront and conquer their anger, ultimately transforming themselves into the most authentic and complete individuals.

The book's strength lies in its practical and actionable solutions, coupled with relatable anecdotes that resonate deeply with readers, allowing them to apply the lessons learned as invaluable guidance in navigating real-life challenges and obstacles. By embracing this book's teachings, readers can not only find effective ways to manage their anger but also unlock their full potential for personal development and growth, leading to a richer and more meaningful life.

CHAPTER 1

TRACK DOWN THE TRIGGERS

A nger is a powerful and complex emotion that, if left unexamined, can disrupt our lives and relationships. Yet, how often do we pause and genuinely understand the triggers that ignite this intense response within us? We often overlook the underlying causes of our anger, attributing it to our inherent nature or external circumstances. However, by diving deep into the exploration of anger triggers, we embark on a transformative journey toward effective anger management and profound self-discovery.

First, we must examine the reasons why you become angry. What is happening in your life that leads to uncontrollable outbursts of anger? Take a moment to reflect on this question. Perhaps there are underlying issues in your life that have gone unaddressed, causing anger to become a default reaction. Consider what lies beneath the surface - the unspoken frustrations, the hurt, the fear, or the sense of powerlessness.

Understanding the triggers that lead to anger goes beyond a mere intellectual exercise; it is an act of introspection and self-awareness. It requires us to peel back the layers of our experiences, beliefs, and emotions to uncover the hidden forces that fuel our fiery reactions. By grasping the intricate web of factors that set off our anger, we gain invaluable insights into ourselves and the influence our internal and external worlds have on our emotional responses.

Envision a world where anger no longer controls us, where we are no longer at the mercy of its whims. By identifying and comprehending our anger triggers, we unlock the power to address the root causes of our emotional turmoil. Suppressing or masking our anger in the hopes that it will dissipate on its own becomes unnecessary. Instead, armed with a profound understanding of our triggers, we can develop healthier coping strategies and chart a path toward emotional well-being.

Lacking this understanding, our attempts to manage anger can become a constant battle against an invisible enemy. We find ourselves trapped in a cycle of reactive outbursts, unresolved conflicts, and strained relationships. Only by delving into the depths of our anger triggers can we break free from this destructive cycle. We acquire the tools to navigate challenging situations with clarity and emotional resilience, paving the way for healthier interactions and more fulfilling connections with others.

Anger is a deeply personal and subjective experience. What triggers intense emotions in one individual may barely register with another. Recognizing this individuality is vital, as it reminds us that we each navigate our unique paths, and it is crucial not to let our emotions dictate our reactions to various situations. Moreover, it is essential to acknowledge that what works effectively for one person in managing their anger may not yield the same results for another. We must embark on a personal journey of self-discovery to explore the strategies and techniques that help us maintain composure and inner calm when faced with upsetting circumstances.

In the realm of anger management, there is no one-size-fits-all solution. The key lies in exploring diverse methods and identifying what resonates most with our unique needs and lifestyles. By embracing a personalized approach to anger management, we empower ourselves to take control of our emotional responses. We become active participants in our wellbeing, equipped with a toolkit of techniques that suit our temperaments and circumstances. This process of self-discovery not only enhances our ability to manage anger but also fosters a deeper understanding of ourselves.

UNRAVELING THE TRIGGERS BEHIND ANGER

Unraveling the triggers behind anger is a crucial step in understanding and effectively managing this powerful emotion. Anger triggers can vary widely from person to person and are influenced by internal and external factors. By exploring and identifying these triggers, individuals gain valuable insights into the underlying causes of their anger, enabling them to develop strategies for coping and responding in healthier ways. This process involves self-reflection, introspection, and a willingness to delve into one's thoughts, emotions, and past experiences.

Internally, triggers for anger can emerge from various factors related to an individual's inner world. Unmet needs, whether physical or emotional, can contribute to feelings of frustration and anger. When our basic needs for safety, belonging, or autonomy are not fulfilled, it can create a sense of powerlessness or injustice, triggering outrage in response to the perceived threat to our well-being. Similarly, unexpressed emotions can build up over time, such as accumulated frustration, disappointment, or hurt, which can serve as underlying triggers for anger. These emotions may surface when a situation or event amplifies unresolved feelings, leading to an angry response.

External factors also play a significant role in triggering anger. Specific events, such as conflicts, criticism, or perceived disrespect, can evoke intense emotional reactions. These triggers often relate to situations where our boundaries are violated or where we feel a threat to our self-esteem or values. For example, a perceived personal attack or unfair treatment can ignite anger in response to feeling disrespected or demeaned. Additionally, environmental factors can contribute to anger triggers. For instance, being in a noisy or crowded environment, facing time pressures, or dealing with challenging circumstances can create a sense of stress or overwhelm that fuels anger.

Anger triggers can be deeply rooted in our past experiences and learned behaviors. Childhood experiences, traumas, and conditioned responses can shape our anger triggers, leading to patterns of reactivity or explosiveness. Unresolved emotional wounds or unprocessed feelings from the past can resurface as triggers in the present, intensifying anger responses. Understanding this connection can help us uncover and heal the underlying issues contributing to our anger triggers.

Additionally, anger can stem from unresolved conflicts and interpersonal issues. Miscommunication, misunderstandings, and differing viewpoints can all contribute to the build-up of conflict within relationships. Also, internal factors such as stress, fatigue, and emotional vulnerability can also contribute to the experience of anger. When we are overwhelmed by external pressures or experiencing heightened emotional states, our tolerance for frustration diminishes, making us more prone to anger outbursts.

Furthermore, it is essential to recognize that anger triggers are not inherently harmful or unjustified. Anger serves as a natural response to perceived threats, injustices, or violations of our boundaries. It can act as a signal that something is not right and motivate us to take action or protect ourselves. However, the way we manage anger is what determines whether it becomes constructive or destructive. Expressing anger in a healthy and constructive manner can motivate individuals to address issues, assert themselves, and bring about positive change.

While external events and circumstances can contribute to anger triggers, it is crucial to emphasize that we have the power to choose our responses. It is not solely the trigger itself that determines our anger but rather our interpretations, beliefs, and coping mechanisms. Developing self-awareness, emotional regulation skills, and effective communication strategies can empower us to navigate anger triggers in healthier and more constructive ways.

ESTABLISHING BOUNDARIES BEFORE ANGER

Establishing clear boundaries is a proactive step in preventing anger from arising in our interactions and relationships. By setting boundaries before anger has a chance to escalate, we create a solid foundation for respectful and harmonious connections. When we communicate our limits and expectations upfront, we allow others to understand and respect our boundaries, reducing the likelihood of anger-triggering situations.

Setting boundaries requires self-awareness and introspection. Reflecting on our values, needs, and triggers helps us identify the areas where boundaries are necessary. By recognizing our limits, we empower ourselves to assertively communicate what we will and will not tolerate, promoting healthier interactions and minimizing the potential for anger to arise.

Open and honest communication is critical in establishing boundaries before anger emerges. Expressing our boundaries assertively and using declarative statements allows us to effectively communicate our needs and expectations without attacking or blaming others. By engaging in respectful dialogue, we encourage understanding and collaboration, fostering an environment where anger triggers are less likely to occur.

In establishing boundaries, we must trust our instincts and listen to our emotions. If a situation or interaction consistently leaves us feeling frustrated, disrespected, or resentful, it may be a sign that our boundaries are being routinely violated. By trusting ourselves and recognizing these emotional cues, we can take the necessary steps to communicate and reinforce our boundaries, preventing anger from escalating and preserving our emotional well-being.

Consistency is a fundamental aspect of boundary establishment. Once we have communicated our boundaries, it is crucial to enforce them consistently. This consistency conveys the message that our boundaries are non-negotiable and deserve respect. By holding firm and setting consequences for boundary violations, we demonstrate that we are committed to maintaining our boundaries, deterring potential anger triggers, and fostering healthier relationships.

Establishing boundaries before anger surfaces requires self-empowerment and self-advocacy. It is an ongoing process that involves self-reflection, effective communication, trust in our instincts, and consistent reinforcement. By taking proactive measures to define and communicate our boundaries, we create an environment of mutual respect and understanding, minimizing the likelihood of anger-triggering situations and promoting our overall emotional well-being.

In the digital age, the internet and social media have opened up new avenues for boundary violations. Cyberbullying, online harassment, and identity theft are all examples of how our digital boundaries can be infiltrated, resulting in feelings of vulnerability, anger, and distress. The online realm offers a sense of anonymity that can embolden individuals to engage in harmful behavior, making it essential for us to establish and enforce clear boundaries to protect ourselves from potential harm.

Setting boundaries and understanding the potential outcomes of boundary violations is crucial for managing anger effectively. By establishing and communicating our boundaries assertively, we establish a framework for healthy and respectful interactions. It empowers us to take control of our lives, reduce stress levels, and cultivate relationships that are built on mutual understanding and respect. To prevent anger from escalating due to boundary violations, individuals can employ the following strategies to establish personal boundaries effectively:

- *Reflect on your values and needs*: Understanding your values, needs, and what you find acceptable in various aspects of life helps you establish boundaries that align with your wellbeing. This self-awareness deters anger triggers by ensuring your boundaries are respected.

- *Communicate assertively*: Clearly and assertively expressing your boundaries to others using declarative statements can prevent anger triggers from arising. Open and honest communication establishes mutual understanding and reduces the chances of boundary violations that may lead to anger.

- *Trust your instincts*: Trusting your instincts is crucial in deterring anger triggers. By paying attention to your levels of discomfort or unease in certain situations or interactions, you can identify potential boundary violations early on and take proactive steps to address them, preventing anger from escalating.

- *Learn to say no*: Setting limits and confidently saying no when something goes against your boundaries or values is a powerful deterrent to anger triggers. By asserting your needs and standing up for yourself, you maintain control over your limits and prevent situations that may lead to anger.

- *Establish consequences*: Clearly communicating the consequences for repeated boundary violations and consistently enforcing them creates a deterrent against anger triggers. When others understand that there are repercussions for crossing your boundaries, they are more likely to respect them, reducing the likelihood of anger-inducing situations.

UNDERSTANDING THE TRIGGERS

Understanding triggers is crucial for managing our emotions, behaviors, and relationships effectively. Triggers are events, situations, or stimuli that evoke a strong emotional or behavioral response within us. These responses can range from anger and anxiety to sadness and fear. By gaining insight into triggers, we can develop self-awareness, emotional intelligence, and better interpersonal skills.

One crucial aspect of understanding triggers is recognizing that they are often rooted in our past experiences and traumas. Triggers can stem from unresolved emotional wounds or painful memories that have shaped our perception of certain situations. For example, a person who has experienced a traumatic event involving dogs may have a trigger response whenever they encounter a barking dog. By understanding the connection between triggers and past experiences, we can begin to unravel the underlying emotions and beliefs associated with them.

Another key aspect is realizing that triggers are subjective and unique to each individual. What may trigger one person may not have the same effect on another. Our personal history, cultural background, and individual sensitivities shape our triggers. It is essential to approach triggers with empathy and respect, recognizing that what may seem insignificant to us could be deeply triggering for someone else. This understanding fosters compassion and helps create a safe and supportive environment for others.

Furthermore, understanding triggers involves learning to differentiate between the trigger event and our response. While we may not control the trigger itself, we can develop strategies to manage our reactions effectively. This may involve techniques such as deep breathing, mindfulness, or seeking support from others. By recognizing our triggers and developing healthy coping mechanisms, we can prevent impulsive or destructive behaviors and make more conscious responses.

Lastly, understanding triggers is an ongoing process that requires self-reflection and self-care. It is not enough to identify our triggers; we must also commit to healing and personal growth. This may involve therapy, self help practices, or engaging in activities that promote emotional well-being. Investing in our emotional health, we can develop resilience and reduce the intensity of our trigger responses over time.

PAST EXPERIENCES PREDICT THE FUTURE

Understanding the relationship between past experiences and future behaviors is crucial when dealing with anger. Past experiences can shape an individual's beliefs, attitudes, and emotional responses, influencing their reactions to triggers. Several important aspects arise from this connection. Our upbringing and experiences, present throughout our lives, shape our identities and responses to situations, with childhood characteristics often persisting into adulthood.

Past experiences serve as the foundation for learned behavior. If someone grew up in an environment where anger was the predominant way of expressing emotions, they might have realized that anger is an acceptable or adequate response. These learned behaviors become ingrained and tend to resurface when triggered by similar situations.

Also, past experiences can create emotional triggers. Traumatic or distressing events in the past can lead to unresolved anger, which acts as a trigger when similar situations arise. For instance, someone who experienced betrayal in a past relationship may become easily angered and defensive when faced with a perceived threat to their trust in subsequent relationships.

Furthermore, past experiences can shape an individual's beliefs and perceptions about themselves and the world around them. If someone has repeatedly experienced powerlessness, rejection, or injustice, they may develop negative core beliefs about themselves or a cynical outlook on others. These beliefs can contribute to a heightened sensitivity to triggers and a tendency to respond with anger as a defense mechanism.

The intensity of past experiences can impact the severity of anger issues. Highly traumatic events, such as physical or emotional abuse, can leave deep emotional scars that take time and professional support to heal. Unresolved trauma often intensifies emotional responses, making it more challenging for individuals to manage their anger in triggering situations.

Recognizing the impact of past experiences on future behaviors is crucial in addressing anger issues. It allows individuals to gain insight into their triggers, identify patterns, and develop healthier coping strategies. By exploring and processing past experiences through therapy, counseling, or support groups, individuals can begin to heal emotional wounds and reframe their beliefs and responses.

Understanding the connection between past experiences and anger responses promotes empathy and self-compassion. It reminds individuals that their anger is often a symptom of unresolved pain rather than a personal failing. This awareness helps individuals respond to triggers with more self-control, allowing them to break free from the cycle of reactive anger and cultivate healthier emotional regulation skills.

FACTORS THAT CONTRIBUTE TO TRIGGERS

Being triggered can be influenced by a multitude of factors that contribute to the intensity and frequency of our emotional reactions. By delving into these critical factors, we can better understand our triggers and develop strategies to manage them more effectively. One of the most influencing factors that contributes to triggering events is the people closest to us. It is often those we have deep emotional connections with, such as family members, partners, or close friends, who have the potential to cause the most pain. Their actions or words hold significant weight in our lives, and when they act in ways that violate our boundaries or disrespect us, it can lead to intense feelings of frustration, hurt, and anger.

For instance, imagine a scenario where a person consistently feels overlooked and unappreciated by their partner. They may communicate their needs and desires, but their partner repeatedly dismisses or invalidates them. Over time, this pattern of neglect can accumulate, and the person might feel angry whenever they perceive similar dismissive behaviors from others. The close relationship dynamic exacerbates the emotional impact, making the trigger more potent and difficult to manage.

Another influential factor lies within our self-destructive tendencies. Negative traits like jealousy, avoidance, neglecting self-care, and engaging in risky behavior can trigger emotional triggers. These negative qualities can take control of our psyche, fueling the flames of anger. When we allow these traits to dominate our thoughts and actions, they become like an endless supply of gasoline, intensifying our emotional reactions and making it challenging to manage our triggers healthily.

For example, consider a person who harbors deep-seated jealousy towards their successful peers. They may constantly compare themselves and feel inadequate, leading to bitterness and resentment. Whenever they encounter situations where others achieve success or receive recognition, it triggers anger within them. Their self-destructive tendency of jealousy amplifies their triggers, hindering their ability to respond calmly and constructively.

Furthermore, past experiences and emotional baggage can significantly contribute to triggering events. Unresolved conflicts, traumatic events, or negative experiences from our past can resurface unexpectedly and provoke intense emotional reactions in the present. These emotional wounds act as triggers, magnifying our anger beyond what may seem proportionate to the current situation.

For instance, someone who experienced a traumatic event in their childhood may find themselves triggered into anger whenever they encounter a situation or person that reminds them of that past trauma. Their emotional response may be disproportionate to the present circumstance, but it stems from the unaddressed pain and unresolved issues associated with the past trauma. Without consciously confronting and working through these experiences, the cycle of anger and frustration persists, and triggers continue to impact their lives.

While each individual's triggers are unique, understanding these key factors provides insight into the patterns that perpetuate triggering events. By analyzing the root causes of our anger, we can identify recurring themes that lead to these triggers. It may involve avoiding certain situations or individuals that consistently provoke our anger or actively working through past traumas and negative experiences that still hold power over us.

To take control of our triggers, we must cultivate self awareness, embrace our vulnerabilities, and discern recurring patterns in our lives. By developing personalized coping mechanisms, such as therapy, mindfulness, or removing ourselves from triggering situations, we can manage triggers effectively. Dedication, consistent effort, and a commitment to personal growth are essential. Through this journey of self-discovery, we can break free from anger and frustration, fostering healthier and more constructive responses to life's challenges.

UNDERSTANDING THE TRIGGERS WITHIN RELATIONSHIPS

Our closest relationships shape our beliefs, values, and behaviors through ongoing interactions and influence. We tend to adopt traits, habits, and even emotional responses from those we spend the most time with. This phenomenon, known as social modeling or social learning, occurs when we observe and imitate the behavior, attitudes, and emotional reactions of our loved ones. As a result of close relationships, we are more likely to exhibit similar traits and triggers as the people closest to us. This can occur through genetic factors, shared environments, and social influences. For example, if a family member or close friend has specific anger triggers, those triggers can become familiar and influential in our lives.

It's important to note that while close relationships can influence our triggers, it doesn't mean those influences solely determine us. We can still develop our emotional regulation skills and make conscious choices about our responses to triggers. By understanding the connection between our triggers and the influences of our loved ones, we can gain insights into our emotional patterns and develop strategies to manage and address them effectively.

Within the dynamics of every relationship, specific individuals possess an uncanny ability to ignite a storm of emotions within us. These are the people who trigger us, who have the power to stir up intense reactions that can quickly escalate into anger or emotional distress. Whether they are close family members, friends, colleagues, or acquaintances, their actions, words, or mere presence can push our buttons and unravel our composure. Exploring the dynamics of these triggering relationships is crucial in understanding ourselves better and finding ways to navigate these interactions with better grace and resilience. In this section, we delve into the complexities of the circumstances and people who trigger us. We examine the underlying issues, potential reasons for their impact, and strategies to maintain emotional equilibrium in their presence.

Family

Family dynamics can have a pervasive influence to ignite triggers for anger, impacting individuals on both a past and present level. It is entirely normal for families to experience problems or dysfunctions at some point in time that do not necessarily revolve around anger-related issues. Families are complex social units with diverse individuals, each with their unique personalities, needs, and challenges. With this being the norm, conflicts, disagreements, and misunderstandings are a natural part of family life. These issues can stem from various sources, such as cultural differences, communication breakdowns, financial stress, parenting challenges, or external factors like work pressures and societal changes.

Unresolved conflicts or past hurts often act as common triggers in family relationships, fueling anger and emotional distress. Within the family unit, individuals share a deep history and emotional bond, making it more likely for unresolved conflicts or past hurts to resurface and impact ongoing dynamics. The accumulation of unresolved conflicts and past hurts can create a sense of resentment, frustration, and anger within family relationships. The emotions associated with these triggers may intensify if left unaddressed, leading to strained interactions, communication breakdowns, and deteriorating trust among family members.

Another trigger within family relationships is the pressure to meet familial expectations or conform to specific roles. Family members may have certain expectations or ideals about how we should live, leading to feelings of pressure, inadequacy, or the need for validation. This can be particularly challenging when our own goals, values, or aspirations do not align with those of our family. These triggers can create conflicts and emotional tension within the family unit. It is crucial to assert our individuality, set healthy boundaries, and communicate our needs and aspirations respectfully and assertively.

Certain family members, given their close familiarity with our triggers and sensitivities developed over shared experiences from childhood to adulthood, may inadvertently enable our anger triggers. They might unknowingly engage in behaviors that worsen anger reactions, either by not addressing the underlying issues or inadvertently provoking us. For instance, they might avoid discussing sensitive topics, thus preventing constructive communication and exacerbating unresolved tensions. While it may not be intentional, this enabling dynamic within the family can perpetuate anger-related issues and hinder the development of healthier coping mechanisms.

Additionally, family relationships can serve as triggers for unresolved childhood wounds or traumas. Instances of neglect, abuse, and trauma during formative years can leave profound emotional wounds, which may manifest as anger and resentment later in life. Growing up in an environment marked by recurring conflict, high-stress levels, or dysfunctional relationships can also contribute to difficulties managing anger. Similarly, someone who endured verbal abuse in their formative years may become highly reactive when faced with criticism or harsh words from family members. Family gatherings or specific family dynamics can evoke memories of past traumatic experiences, leading to intense emotional reactions, such as anger, anxiety, or a sense of powerlessness.

While anger-related problems are one potential aspect, families may also face issues like lack of communication, emotional distance, trust issues, or coping with significant life transitions. Unaddressed anger-related problems can lead to emotional turmoil, conflicts, and strained relationships within families and other social circles. Families must recognize that facing challenges is normal and does not mean failure. Open communication, empathy, and a willingness to address problems together can lead to growth and understanding, ultimately strengthening the family bond.

Problems

The dynamics within a family can be a complex web of interactions, emotions, and challenges. While families are often a source of love, support, and security, they can also be the breeding ground for various problems that affect the well-being and harmony of their members. These problems may arise from communication breakdowns, unresolved conflicts, power struggles, role expectations, emotional neglect, substance abuse, or transfer of unresolved trauma. Understanding and addressing these issues are essential for cultivating healthier family dynamics, fostering stronger relationships, and nurturing an environment where all members can thrive and find emotional fulfillment. The following problems are commonly pervasive in many families and can often lead to triggering anger.

- *Communication Issues*: Ineffective or dysfunctional communication patterns can lead to misunderstandings, misinterpretations, and unresolved conflicts, causing frustration and anger within the family.

- *Unresolved Conflicts*: Lingering unresolved conflicts can create a constant source of tension, erupting into anger during future interactions among family members.

- *Lack of Boundaries*: Difficulties establishing and respecting personal boundaries can result in feelings of intrusion, disrespect, and resentment, triggering anger within the family unit.

- *Power Imbalance*: Power struggles and an imbalance of authority within the family can provoke anger and resentment when one family member dominates decision-making or exercises control over others.

- *Past Trauma or Unresolved Issues*: Unresolved past trauma or unresolved issues from the past can resurface during family interactions, triggering anger and emotional turmoil as painful memories and unresolved conflicts resurface.

Solutions

Recognizing the uniqueness of each family situation is crucial, as there is no universal solution for addressing complicated family dynamics. However, with the proper support and resources, it is possible to strive toward a healthier and more positive family dynamic. The well-being and safety of all family members should be the foremost concern, coupled with establishing effective communication channels and a willingness to seek help when needed. While navigating these challenges, families can consider a range of solutions, including seeking professional guidance through therapy or counseling, setting clear boundaries, involving neutral mediators if conflicts seem insurmountable, and prioritizing personal growth and self-care. By approaching these strategies listed with patience, empathy, and a commitment to positive change, families can work towards fostering stronger, more harmonious relationships.

- *Effective Communication*: Open, honest, and respectful communication is vital for resolving conflicts and preventing misunderstandings that can trigger anger. Active listening, using declarative statements, and expressing emotions and needs clearly can promote understanding and reduce tension.

- *Conflict Resolution Skills*: Learning and practicing effective conflict resolution strategies, such as negotiation, compromise, and problem-solving, can help family members address disagreements constructively. This approach encourages collaboration, empathy, and finding mutually satisfactory solutions.

- *Emotional Regulation Techniques*: Developing skills to manage and regulate emotions is crucial for preventing anger from escalating. Techniques like deep breathing, mindfulness, journaling, and seeking support from therapy or counseling can help individuals cope with anger triggers and respond in a more controlled and calm manner.

- *Establishing Boundaries*: Setting and respecting personal boundaries is essential in maintaining healthy family dynamics. Clearly defining boundaries, communicating them assertively, and enforcing them when necessary helps prevent misunderstandings, conflicts, and resentment.

- *Family Therapy*: Seeking professional help through family therapy can provide a safe and supportive space for exploring and resolving deep-rooted issues. A trained therapist can facilitate open communication, offer valuable insights, and guide the family in developing healthier patterns of interaction. Family therapy can help address underlying dynamics, improve relationships, and provide tools for effective anger management.

Friends

The friends we associate with often reflect our ideologies and characteristics, as famously stated by Jim Rohn: "You are the average of the five people you spend the most time with." Essentially, this means that the traits and behaviors of those closest to us tend to influence us. Unlike family members with whom we share a lineage, we can consciously select our friends. As friendships develop, they become integral to our lives, with an inherent understanding of how we function. Friends play a vital role in our personal growth and development, supporting us through life's challenges and inspiring us to become better versions of ourselves.

When we spend time with our friends, we are not only sharing enjoyable moments but also witnessing their actions, attitudes, and reactions to different situations. During this process, we may encounter certain behaviors or responses from our friends that deeply resonate with us and elicit a strong emotional reaction. For example, if a friend consistently displays aggressive behavior or reacts angrily in certain situations, it may trigger feelings of unease or discomfort within us, especially if we have experienced similar problems. These reactions can trigger our sensitivities and bring forth emotions or memories that we may have suppressed or not fully addressed.

While friendships are an essential part of our lives, they are not exempt from problems. One common trigger in friendships is betrayal or a breach of trust. When a friend acts in a way that goes against our values or expectations, such as sharing a secret or spreading rumors, it can lead to feelings of hurt, anger, or disappointment. These triggers can strain the friendship and may require open and honest communication to address the issue, rebuild trust, and restore the relationship.

Another trigger within friendships can be differences in values, beliefs, or interests. As individuals, we have unique perspectives and preferences that may not always align with those of our friends. Disagreements or clashes on important matters can lead to tension and emotional triggers. Additionally, changes in circumstances or life stages can trigger emotional responses in friendships. Life is dynamic, and people naturally evolve and go through different phases. When friends experience significant life changes, such as moving to a new city, starting a family, or pursuing other career paths, it can create a sense of distance or unease. These triggers can evoke feelings of sadness, jealousy, or fear of abandonment.

Problems

Friendships, while often a source of joy and support, are not immune to problems that can trigger anger. Some common issues can arise within friendships, leading to emotional turmoil and strained relationships. These problems include trust issues, betrayal, lack of communication, unresolved conflicts, differing values or opinions, jealousy, and neglect. When these issues are left unaddressed or mishandled, they can escalate into intense feelings of anger, resentment, and even the breakdown of the friendship. It is crucial to recognize and understand these pervasive problems to navigate them and maintain healthy and fulfilling friendships effectively.

- *Betrayal*: Betrayal occurs when a friend breaks trust by lying, spreading rumors, or sharing personal information without permission. This breach of trust can trigger anger as it violates the foundation of the friendship and leads to feelings of hurt and betrayal.
- *Lack of Communication*: Poor communication or a lack of open and honest dialogue can create misunderstandings and misinterpretations. When friends fail to communicate effectively, it can lead to frustration, resentment, and unresolved conflicts, ultimately triggering anger.
- *Unresolved Conflicts*: Unresolved conflicts can fester and escalate, causing tension and anger in the friendship. When disagreements or grievances are not addressed and resolved through healthy

communication and compromise, they can lead to ongoing bitterness and resentment.

- *Differing Values or Opinions*: Friends may have different values, beliefs, or opinions, sometimes leading to disagreements and clashes. When these differences are not acknowledged or respected, it can cause frustration, anger, and a sense of being misunderstood or invalidated.

- *Jealousy and Envy*: Feelings of jealousy and envy can arise when one friend perceives the other as more successful, attractive, or accomplished. These emotions can trigger resentment and anger, leading to strained relationships. Unhealthy competition and comparison can further exacerbate these negative emotions.

Solutions

Friendships are invaluable connections we nurture and cherish, offering mutual support, joy, and shared experiences. Yet, even the closest friendships can face challenges that trigger anger and strain the bond. The good news is that there are practical and effective solutions to maintain and enhance the strength of these valuable relationships. It's crucial to recognize that each friendship is unique, requiring adaptable approaches to address specific dynamics and individual needs. Through open communication, setting boundaries, resolving conflicts, practicing empathy, and cultivating forgiveness, we can develop and sustain the beneficial friendships that enrich our lives. By implementing these strategies, we can prevent anger from causing lasting damage and promote growth of healthier and more fulfilling friendships.

- *Open and Honest Communication*: Establishing a foundation of open and honest communication is crucial for resolving conflicts and maintaining healthy friendships. Encourage open dialogue, active listening, and the expression of thoughts and feelings in a non-judgmental manner. Clear communication helps address misunderstandings and promotes understanding and empathy.

- *Setting Boundaries*: Establishing and respecting personal boundaries is essential in maintaining healthy friendships. Communicate your boundaries and expectations to your friends and encourage them to do the same. Respecting each other's boundaries fosters mutual respect, reduces conflicts, and promotes a healthier dynamic.

- *Conflict Resolution*: Learning effective conflict resolution skills is vital for resolving disagreements and preventing anger from escalating. Encourage calm and respectful discussions, actively listen to each other's perspectives, and seek common ground. Finding compromises and solutions together can strengthen the friendship and prevent resentment from building.

- *Practicing Empathy and Understanding*: Cultivating empathy and understanding towards your friend's experiences and emotions helps create a supportive and compassionate environment. Put yourself in their shoes, validate their feelings, and try to understand their perspective. This promotes emotional connection and fosters a more profound bond within the friendship.

- *Cultivating Forgiveness*: Forgiveness is a powerful tool in repairing and maintaining friendships. Holding onto anger and grudges can strain relationships and hinder personal growth. Practice forgiveness by letting go of past hurts, understanding that everyone makes mistakes, and working towards healing and rebuilding trust.

Partner/Significant Other

Intimate relationships can be a source of deep connection, love, and support, but they can also bring forth various triggers that can challenge our emotional well-being. These triggers often arise from past experiences, unresolved issues, or unmet needs, and they can significantly impact the dynamics of the relationship. One common trigger in intimate relationships is communication breakdown. When communication becomes strained or ineffective, misunderstandings, misinterpretations, and conflicts can quickly arise, leading to emotional distress and frustration.

Additionally, past traumas or emotional wounds can resurface within intimate relationships, triggering feelings of fear, vulnerability, or insecurity. These triggers can be activated by certain words, behaviors, or even subtle cues from our partner. It is crucial to recognize and address these triggers with open and honest communication, empathy, and a willingness to understand each other's perspectives.

Another common trigger in intimate relationships is the fear of abandonment or rejection. This fear may stem from past experiences of feeling abandoned, betrayed, or unloved, and it can manifest in different ways within the relationship. The fear of being left or rejected can lead to clinginess, possessiveness, or a constant need for reassurance, which can strain the relationship and create a cycle of emotional turmoil.

Also, intimacy itself can serve as a trigger for some individuals. Opening up emotionally and being vulnerable with a partner can evoke discomfort, fear of judgment, or past emotional wounds. This vulnerability trigger can create a barrier to deeper emotional connection and hinder the growth of the relationship.

Problems

Intimate relationships can encounter problems for various reasons, stemming from the unique complexities and dynamics between partners. One common factor is the inherent differences between individuals, including contrasting communication styles, emotional needs, and personal values. These differences can sometimes lead to misunderstandings, conflicts, and challenges in meeting each other's expectations. When partners have different desires, goals, or levels of emotional support, it can lead to frustration or feelings of dissatisfaction. These triggers can escalate into conflicts or cause emotional distancing.

External stressors such as work pressures, financial difficulties, or family obligations can also strain the relationship, affecting the emotional well-being of both partners. Furthermore, unresolved issues from the past, such as past traumas or unresolved conflicts, can resurface and impact the current relationship, triggering emotional responses and challenges. Here are some of the most prevalent and pervasive problems that occur within relationships:

- *Communication breakdown*: Effective communication is the foundation of a healthy relationship. When communication breaks down, misunderstandings occur, and conflicts can escalate. Poor communication can lead to frustration, resentment, and a lack of emotional connection between partners.

- *Trust issues*: Trust forms the core of a solid and fulfilling relationship. However, trust is eroded by betrayal, infidelity, or dishonesty. Once trust is broken, it can be challenging to rebuild, leading to ongoing tension, insecurity, and anger.

- *Conflict and disagreements*: Disagreements and conflicts are natural in any relationship, but unresolved or recurring conflicts can strain the relationship. Constant arguments, power struggles, or the inability to resolve differences can escalate anger and resentment between partners.

- *Emotional or physical neglect*: Emotional and physical neglect occurs when one partner fails to provide the necessary emotional support, affection, or attention. Neglect can leave the other partner feeling unimportant and unloved and lead to anger, loneliness, and dissatisfaction within the relationship.

- *Differences in expectations and needs*: Partners may have different expectations, desires, and needs within a relationship. When these differences are not addressed and understood, it can result in unmet expectations, disappointment, and frustration. Clashes in priorities, goals, or values can also create ongoing tension and conflict.

Solutions

Finding effective solutions is crucial for partners dealing with problems within relationships as it provides an opportunity to restore harmony, strengthen the bond, and promote a healthier connection. Ignoring or avoiding problems can lead to resentment, unresolved conflicts, and further deterioration of the relationship. By actively seeking solutions, couples can address the root causes of their issues, improve communication, rebuild trust, and create a more supportive and fulfilling partnership.

Implementing solutions allows partners to navigate challenges, enhance their understanding of each other's needs, and work together towards a shared vision of a loving and resilient relationship. It requires commitment, empathy, and a willingness to grow individually and as a couple. By embracing solutions, couples can cultivate a relationship that thrives on mutual respect, effective communication, and a genuine desire to overcome obstacles together. Partners need to adapt these strategies to their specific circumstances and be willing to invest time, effort, and patience into implementing them.

- *Open and Honest Communication*: Effective communication is the foundation of a healthy relationship. Partners should actively listen to each other, express their thoughts and feelings clearly and respectfully, and be open to constructive feedback. By promoting open and honest communication, couples can address issues directly, clarify misunderstandings, and work towards finding mutually beneficial solutions.

- *Active Listening and Empathy*: Understanding and empathizing with your partner's perspective is essential for resolving conflicts. Active listening involves giving your full attention, validating your partner's emotions, and seeking to understand their point of view. Empathy lets you put yourself in their shoes, fostering compassion and a deeper connection. This approach enables mutual understanding, promotes empathy, and paves the way for finding common ground.

- *Conflict Resolution and Problem-Solving*: Conflict is inevitable in any relationship, but it's how couples handle and resolve it that makes a difference. Implementing effective conflict resolution techniques, such as identifying underlying issues, brainstorming solutions, and compromising, enables partners to work through disagreements respectfully and productively. Problem-solving skills allow couples to collaborate and find solutions that meet both partners' needs.

- *Rebuild Trust*: Trust forms the core of a strong partnership. If trust has been compromised, it is crucial to focus on rebuilding it. This may involve open discussions about trust issues, setting clear boundaries, and following through on commitments. Building trust takes time, patience, and consistent actions demonstrating reliability and transparency.

- *Seek Professional Help*: In some cases, professional assistance can benefit couples facing complex or deeply rooted problems. Seeking couples' therapy or relationship counseling provides a structured and neutral environment for partners to explore their issues, learn effective communication techniques, and gain insights into their dynamics. A trained therapist can offer guidance, facilitate productive conversations, and provide tools to help couples navigate challenges and foster long-term relationship growth.

Parenting

Parenting is a multifaceted journey filled with love, nurturing, and guidance, but it also entails worry, sacrifice, and struggle. It is an emotional roller coaster where moments of joy and fulfillment coexist with anger, frustration, and doubt. As children grow, parenting challenges evolve, and behaviors like tantrums, defiance, and pushing boundaries can trigger parental anger. It can be challenging to witness children developing their individual identities and disregarding rules. However, it's important to remember that anger is not the solution. Allowing anger to prevail can damage the parent-child relationship, undermine authority, and leave the child afraid and hurt.

Additionally, the demands of parenting can lead to feelings of resentment, as the stress and responsibilities consume time and energy. Despite these challenges, it's crucial to recognize that they are a natural part of parenting. Reconnecting with the initial reasons for becoming a parent and embracing these challenges as opportunities for personal growth and learning can help navigate the complexities of parenting. By approaching the relationship with love, patience, and guidance, parents can foster a nurturing environment and build a strong bond with their children.

Problems

As parents strive to provide the best for their children, the demands of parenting can be overwhelming. From sleepless nights and constant worry to balancing work and family responsibilities, stress can affect parents' emotional well-being. Children naturally go through different stages of development, testing boundaries, asserting independence, and exhibiting challenging behaviors. These moments can ignite frustration and anger as parents try to find effective ways to discipline, communicate, and connect with their children.

One prevalent trigger in parenting is the feeling of inadequacy or the fear of failing as a parent. The immense responsibility of raising and nurturing a child can lead to self-doubt, guilt, or anxiety. Parents may feel triggered when they perceive themselves as falling short or comparing themselves to others. Another common trigger in parenting is the clash of expectations and differing parenting styles. When parents have different beliefs, values, or approaches to parenting, it can lead to conflicts and triggers within the relationship. Disagreements about discipline, routines, or decision making can create tension and emotional reactions.

Parents may feel triggered when they are unable to meet all the expectations or when they struggle to find a balance between their own needs and those of their children. Triggers can also arise from unresolved childhood wounds or past traumas that resurface within the context of parenting. Parenting can bring up memories, fears, or unresolved emotions from one's upbringing, triggering emotional reactions and patterns.

Parenting comes with its fair share of challenges, and it's important to acknowledge that anger can be a natural response to these difficulties. However, by recognizing the triggers, seeking support when needed, and implementing effective communication and coping strategies, parents can cultivate a healthier relationship with their children. It's crucial to understand that every family is unique, and the factors that trigger anger may vary. By addressing these prevalent issues head-on, parents can navigate their challenges more effectively, creating an environment that nurtures understanding, empathy, and love for both parents and children.

- *Discipline and Behavior*: One of the most prevalent issues in parenting is dealing with discipline and behavior problems. Children may exhibit challenging behaviors such as defiance, tantrums, or disobedience, which can frustrate and trigger anger in parents. It becomes a source of conflict when parents struggle to find effective discipline strategies or when they feel overwhelmed by their child's behavior.

- *Lack of Communication*: Communication breakdown between parents and children can lead to misunderstandings, frustration, and pent-up anger. Parents may struggle to effectively communicate their expectations or concerns, while children may have difficulty expressing their emotions or understanding parental instructions. This breakdown in communication can create a gap between parents and children, leading to feelings of anger and resentment.

- *Parental Stress and Overwhelm*: Parenting can be demanding and stressful, with multiple responsibilities and limited time for self-care. The constant juggling of work, household tasks, and childcare can leave parents feeling overwhelmed and exhausted. When stress levels rise, parents may be more prone to anger, as they struggle to manage their own emotions while attending to their children's needs.

- *Differences in Parenting Styles*: Parenting styles can vary between parents, which can lead to conflicts and trigger anger. When partners have different approaches to parenting, disagreements may arise regarding discipline methods, decision-making, or setting boundaries. These differences can create tension and undermine the unity and consistency in parenting, causing frustration and anger.

- *Unrealistic Expectations*: Unrealistic expectations can set the stage for frustration and anger in parenting. Parents may have idealized notions of what their child should be like or how their parenting journey should unfold. When reality doesn't align with these expectations, it can lead to disappointment, resentment, and feelings of failure, triggering anger in parents.

Solutions

Balancing anger management while raising a child and nurturing a healthy relationship with your partner can be a complex endeavor. However, there are proven strategies and solutions that can assist parents in navigating these challenges and fostering a harmonious family dynamic. By incorporating techniques, parents can maintain a nurturing environment for their children and cultivate a robust and intimate connection with their partner. These strategies aim to provide practical solutions for parents to cope with anger issues:

- *Anger Awareness*: The first step in managing anger as a parent is to develop an awareness of your triggers and emotional responses. Reflect on situations that provoke anger and identify the underlying reasons for your reactions. This self-awareness will help you better understand your emotions and respond more effectively.

- *Emotional Regulation Techniques*: Once you're aware of your triggers, it's crucial to develop techniques for emotional regulation. Deep breathing exercises, mindfulness practices, and relaxation techniques can help you calm down in moments of frustration. Taking a pause, stepping away from the situation briefly, and giving yourself time to cool down can prevent anger from escalating.

- *Effective Communication*: Clear and open communication is vital in preventing misunderstandings and conflicts leading to anger. Practice active listening, empathy, and expressing your thoughts and concerns assertively rather than aggressively. Parents need to have open dialogue amongst each other and their children to ensure expectations are properly met and rules are established. This creates greater understanding and trust while strengthening the family bond.

- *Establish Boundaries and Consistent Discipline*: Setting clear boundaries and expectations for behavior is crucial in preventing anger triggers. Consistent discipline techniques, such as positive reinforcement, logical consequences, and age-appropriate rules, provide a structured environment for your child. This consistency helps reduce frustration and promotes a sense of security for both parent and child.

- *Self-Care and Support*: Parenting can be overwhelming and taking care of yourself is essential for managing anger. Prioritize self-care activities that help you relax, recharge, and maintain a positive mindset. Seek support from friends, family, or parenting groups to share experiences, gain perspective, and receive guidance during challenging times.

In conclusion, understanding our triggers and working on our emotional responses is not a one-time endeavor; it requires continuous dedication and practice. By consistently applying these strategies, especially in our interactions with those closest to us, we can pave the way for a more peaceful and fulfilling life, fostering deeper connections and a greater sense of inner peace and contentment.

Loved ones, being the closest to us, often play a significant role in our emotional landscape. Therefore, applying these principles within those relationships can lead to transformative results. As we navigate interactions with family and friends who trigger us, let us remind ourselves of the opportunity for growth and personal development that lies before us. Instead of reacting impulsively, we can pause, reflect, and choose healthier responses that promote understanding and compassion.

Taking responsibility for our emotional reactions is paramount. Instead of blaming or avoiding the people who trigger us, let us embrace the challenge of self-reflection and personal growth. Consistency is critical in applying these strategies. Every time we encounter individuals who have the potential to ignite anger, we should be mindful of our reactions and seek to transform them. By delving into the key aspects of these triggers, we gain valuable insights into ourselves and our vulnerabilities. This deeper understanding empowers us to work on our emotional responses and develop inner strength and resilience.

INTERNAL TRIGGERS

Internal triggers play a significant role in the manifestation and management of anger. These triggers encompass a range of internal factors, including emotions, beliefs, and past experiences, which influence our perception and response to anger-provoking situations. Emotions such as frustration, fear, and hurt can intensify anger and contribute to impulsive reactions. It is crucial to recognize and acknowledge these emotions, allowing ourselves to experience and process them in healthy ways. This can involve practices like mindfulness, deep breathing, or engaging in activities that promote emotional well-being, such as journaling or talking to a trusted confidant.

In addition to emotions, our beliefs also shape our experience of anger. Deep-rooted beliefs formed through upbringing, societal conditioning, or personal experiences can significantly impact how we interpret and respond to anger triggers. Identifying these underlying beliefs is essential for effective anger management. We must challenge and reframe negative or irrational thoughts that contribute to anger. This process involves questioning the validity of these beliefs, seeking evidence to the contrary, and replacing them with more constructive and rational perspectives.

Past experiences, particularly unresolved traumas or adverse events, can influence our anger responses. Unaddressed emotional wounds may resurface during anger-provoking situations, amplifying the intensity of our reactions. To effectively process anger and manage its triggers, it is crucial to address and heal from past traumas. Seeking professional therapy or counseling can provide a supportive and safe environment for exploring these experiences and developing healthy coping mechanisms.

Processing and managing anger triggers require self awareness and a commitment to personal growth. It involves understanding and acknowledging the role of internal stimuli, such as emotions, beliefs, and past experiences, in shaping our anger responses. By cultivating emotional intelligence, challenging negative beliefs, and addressing unresolved traumas, we can develop healthier ways of processing and managing anger. This journey of self-discovery and healing empowers individuals to respond to anger triggers more constructively and mindfully, leading to improved relationships and overall well-being.

SITUATIONAL TRIGGERS

Life can often feel like a treacherous journey, where unexpected triggers lie in wait, ready to ignite our emotions. Situational triggers encompass conflicts, arguments, criticism, rejection, feeling overwhelmed or stressed, experiencing loss or disappointment, and encountering problems that challenge our values or expectations. Additionally, internal emotional states, such as feeling dismissed, neglected, or inadequate, can further intensify frustration and anger. These triggers can become even more potent when they tap into past traumas, resurfacing when we perceive a threat in our environment. It's as if a switch is flipped, and suddenly, we find ourselves overwhelmed with intense emotions that seem beyond our control.

While anger is a universal emotion experienced by everyone, some individuals struggle with chronic anger that significantly disrupts their daily lives. The root cause of anger often lies in external situational and environmental triggers. One of the most prevalent triggers is stress, which can stem from various sources, such as demanding work pressures, financial struggles, or relationship conflicts. As stress accumulates, it becomes a breeding ground for frustration and irritability, quickly escalating into full-blown anger.

Traumatic experiences also serve as potent triggers for anger issues, leaving deep emotional wounds that can manifest as anger. Whether it's the aftermath of abuse, the impact of accidents, or the scars left by natural disasters, traumas can significantly affect an individual's ability to manage anger, primarily if these traumatic events occurred during childhood.

Situational triggers can vary in terms of control, and it depends on the circumstances and individual factors. Some situational triggers may be beyond a person's immediate control, as they arise from unexpected events or the actions of others. For example, someone may experience frustration and anger when encountering heavy traffic on their commute.

Similarly, encountering rude or disrespectful behavior from others can trigger anger, even though the individual has no control over someone else's actions.

In the face of these situational triggers, it's essential to recognize that complete avoidance or disassociation from negative people or uncomfortable situations may not always be feasible. Triggers are an inevitable part of life, requiring us to develop effective strategies to cope with them. By identifying our triggers, we can cultivate coping mechanisms that empower us to navigate our emotions more skillfully.

Trauma

Dealing with trauma can profoundly impact how we experience and respond to anger triggers. Traumatic experiences, such as abuse, accidents, or significant losses, can leave deep emotional wounds that linger within us. These wounds become sensitive points easily triggered by specific situations or stimuli, leading to intense anger reactions. When unresolved trauma is present, our emotional response to even minor stressors or conflicts can be disproportionately heightened. It's as if the trauma acts as a lens through which we perceive and interpret the world, amplifying our anger response and making it difficult to regulate our emotions effectively.

The effects of trauma on triggering anger are multifaceted. Trauma can disrupt our sense of safety, trust, and self-worth, leaving us vulnerable and on edge. It can also distort our perception of current events, causing us to interpret neutral or benign situations as threatening or dangerous. This hyper-arousal can lead to a constant state of vigilance, where individuals are primed to react defensively or aggressively to perceived threats. Additionally, traumatic experiences can erode our coping mechanisms, leaving us with limited emotional resources to manage anger triggers effectively. This combination of heightened reactivity, distorted perception, and diminished coping skills creates a perfect storm for anger to emerge and intensify.

Bullying

Bullying is a pervasive issue that can significantly impact triggering anger in individuals. When someone experiences bullying, whether it occurs in childhood, adolescence, or even adulthood, it can profoundly affect their emotional well-being and how they manage anger. The relentless and targeted nature of bullying can create feelings of powerlessness, humiliation, and injustice, which can fuel anger responses.

Victims of bullying often endure repeated acts of aggression, verbal abuse, and social exclusion, which can erode their self-esteem and self-worth. The constant stress and fear associated with bullying can lead to heightened anger and irritability as individuals struggle to cope with the emotional and psychological toll it takes on them.

Furthermore, bullying can leave lasting emotional scars, impacting how individuals perceive themselves and others. It can create a heightened sensitivity to potential triggers, making individuals more prone to reacting with anger when they perceive a threat or mistreatment. The emotional pain inflicted by bullying can become deeply ingrained, making it difficult to trust others and increasing the likelihood of defensive and hostile responses in various situations.

The long-term effects of bullying can extend beyond the immediate experience. Individuals who have been bullied may develop negative beliefs about themselves and others, such as feeling unworthy, unlovable, or constantly expecting mistreatment. These deep-rooted beliefs can trigger anger, as individuals may perceive situations as confirming their negative self-perceptions or reinforcing the idea that the world is hostile and unkind.

Abuse and Neglect

The effects of abuse and neglect can have profound and long-lasting consequences triggering anger responses in individuals. Abuse, whether physical, emotional, or sexual, inflicts deep wounds that can erode a person's sense of self-worth, trust, and safety. Survivors of abuse often carry unresolved anger and resentment stemming from the violation of their boundaries and the betrayal of trust by those who were supposed to protect them. The experience of neglect, where one's basic physical and emotional needs are consistently unmet, can also lead to anger as individuals struggle with feelings of abandonment, rejection, and a sense of not being valued or cared for.

When individuals who have experienced abuse or neglect encounter situations that remind them of their past trauma, it can trigger a cascade of anger and intense emotions. These triggers may vary from person to person, but common examples include feeling disregarded, criticized, or controlled or experiencing situations that threaten their safety or autonomy. The unaddressed anger resulting from abuse and neglect can manifest in different ways, such as explosive outbursts, passive-aggressive behavior, or a constant simmering anger that colors their interactions and relationships.

The effects of abuse and neglect are far-reaching, affecting both the individual's emotional well-being and their overall physical health. These experiences often occur alongside other forms of mistreatment, such as substance abuse, domestic violence, and child maltreatment, intensifying the trauma endured. Individuals who have experienced abuse and neglect may suffer from a range of physical and mental health issues, including heightened stress levels, hypertension, depression, and even thoughts of suicide. These challenges can lead to social isolation and difficulties in managing daily life.

Financial Crisis

Living in poverty can have profound effects on triggering anger. The daily struggles and hardships associated with poverty, such as financial insecurity, limited access to resources, and social inequalities, can generate stress and frustration. The inability to meet basic needs and provide for oneself and loved ones can lead to feelings of powerlessness, shame, and resentment. Additionally, the experience of witnessing others living in abundance while being trapped in poverty can evoke a sense of injustice and fuel anger. The chronic stressors and persistent challenges of poverty can erode an individual's emotional well-being and coping mechanisms, increasing the likelihood of anger outbursts and difficulties in managing anger effectively.

Lack of financial resources also creates a cycle of intergenerational trauma and anger. Children growing up in impoverished environments may witness and experience the effects of poverty-related stress, which can shape their emotional development and coping strategies. The lack of access to quality education, healthcare, and opportunities for personal growth can further exacerbate frustration and anger. As a result, individuals who have experienced poverty may carry these anger triggers into adulthood, perpetuating a cycle of anger and frustration within their families and communities. Poverty exposes individuals to daily conflicts and threats, including violence, crime, and community instability. These circumstances can significantly exacerbate anger management issues, further challenging individuals in their ability to navigate and regulate their emotions effectively.

While not all impoverished families exhibit extremely negative social traits, a combination of various factors can create a challenging environment. The experience of poverty can contribute to mental health problems, including depression, anxiety, and anger issues. Anger triggered by deprivation is a valid response to challenging circumstances. Anger is a natural emotional reaction to these adversities, signaling a need for change and addressing the underlying systemic issues perpetuating poverty. The daily struggles and persistent stressors experienced in poverty can create a sense of frustration, powerlessness, and injustice. Validating the anger of impoverished individuals acknowledges their lived experiences and the impact of socio-economic factors on their well-being.

SOLUTIONS FOR SITUATIONAL TRIGGERS

Dealing with situational triggers can indeed be a challenging aspect of life but embracing these experiences as learning opportunities can lead to personal growth and empowerment. Avoiding situations out of fear of triggering anger responses can limit our experiences and hinder our ability to develop effective coping strategies. When we approach triggers with curiosity rather than avoidance, we open ourselves up to understanding our emotional responses and behavioral patterns better. By delving into the root causes of our triggers, we gain valuable insights into our fears, insecurities, and unresolved emotions.

Experience serves as a profound teacher, and as we navigate through triggering situations, we can fine-tune our coping strategies. Controlled and safe exposure to triggers can foster resilience, but it is crucial to embrace this process gradually and with self-compassion. Pushing ourselves too aggressively may prove counterproductive, potentially triggering overwhelming emotional responses. Instead, by incrementally confronting our triggers, we allow ourselves the necessary space to learn and grow at a pace that aligns with our emotional well-being. Each encounter becomes a step toward greater emotional strength, providing valuable insights into our triggers and teaching us how to manage and navigate them in the future effectively.

Building a versatile toolbox of coping strategies ensures we have multiple approaches to draw upon when facing various triggers. What works for one situation may not be as effective in another, so having a range of techniques can offer flexibility and adaptability. Cultivating mindfulness practices can be immensely beneficial in dealing with situational triggers. Techniques such as meditation, deep breathing exercises, or mindfulness-based stress reduction can help us stay present in the moment and respond to triggers with a greater sense of clarity and calmness. This toolbox may include cognitive reframing, positive affirmations, grounding exercises, or engaging in creative outlets as a means of emotional expression.

One practical, real-life solution for managing situational triggers is to practice self-awareness and reflection. By observing our emotional reactions and identifying the specific triggers, we gain valuable insights into the underlying reasons for our responses. Journaling or taking moments of quiet contemplation can help us understand the patterns and emotions connected to these triggers. Through this process of self-discovery, we can develop a deeper understanding of ourselves and our triggers, which lays the foundation for crafting personalized coping mechanisms.

Seeking guidance from mentors, support groups, or mental health professionals is a constructive approach to dealing with situational triggers. Engaging with individuals who have confronted similar challenges or possess expertise in emotional management can offer invaluable perspectives and coping techniques. By learning from the experiences of others, we gain fresh insights and innovative strategies that might have eluded us on our own. This collaborative approach reinforces the notion that we are not alone in our struggles and that shared wisdom can be a powerful tool for personal growth. Embracing the support of others allows us to tap into a wealth of knowledge and understanding, empowering us to navigate triggering situations with newfound strength and resilience.

Documenting the situations, events, or individuals that trigger our anger is a powerful and valuable strategy for managing this intense emotion. When we put our thoughts and experiences into writing, we transform abstract feelings into a tangible form, providing us with an opportunity for profound self-reflection and self-awareness. Through this practice, we begin to acknowledge and understand the root causes of our anger, including underlying frustrations or past traumas that may influence our emotional responses. This heightened self-awareness is instrumental in developing effective coping strategies tailored to our specific triggers.

When triggers evoke intense emotional reactions, they can disrupt our ability to function effectively in various aspects of life, affecting relationships, work, and personal growth. By developing effective strategies, we grant ourselves the means to navigate triggering situations with resilience and emotional balance. These strategies provide us with invaluable tools to understand and manage our triggers, allowing us to respond in healthier and more adaptive ways. By proactively addressing our triggers, we break free from the cycle of reactivity and cultivate a profound sense of empowerment and control over our emotions and life experiences.

While the importance and effectiveness of strategies may vary depending on the individual and their specific circumstances, here are the most effective techniques that can help individuals overcome situational triggers:

- *Self-awareness*: Developing self-awareness is crucial in identifying and understanding one's emotional triggers. By recognizing the thoughts, feelings, and physical sensations that arise in triggering situations, individuals can gain insight into their reactions and begin to make conscious choices about their responses.

- *Cognitive reframing*: Cognitive reframing involves challenging and reframing negative thoughts and beliefs contributing to anger triggers. By replacing distorted or unhelpful thinking patterns with more balanced and rational thoughts, individuals can alter their perspectives and reduce the intensity of their emotional reactions.

- *Stress management*: Implementing effective techniques can significantly reduce the likelihood of anger triggers. Engaging in regular exercise, practicing relaxation techniques such as deep breathing or meditation, and adopting healthy lifestyle habits can help individuals better cope with stressors and maintain emotional balance.

- *Communication skills*: Enhancing communication skills can significantly improve interpersonal relationships and prevent or diffuse triggering situations. Active listening, assertiveness, and conflict resolution techniques enable individuals to express their needs, boundaries, and concerns respectfully and constructively, reducing the likelihood of anger escalation.

- *Support systems*: Building a solid support system is vital for managing situational triggers. Surrounding oneself with trusted friends, family members, or support groups provide an outlet for sharing experiences, seeking guidance, and receiving emotional support. Connecting with others who have faced similar challenges can provide validation and perspective, reinforcing the belief that one is not alone in their journey.

REFLECTION

Anger is an overwhelming emotion that can easily lead us astray if left unchecked. Its impulsive nature often tempts us to react without considering the consequences, causing regrettable outcomes. However, by acknowledging the power of our reactions and the significance they hold in our lives, we can learn to control our anger effectively. It is essential to recognize that we cannot control every situation or the actions of others. Accepting this reality becomes a necessary aspect of managing our anger, allowing us to respond with greater clarity and composure.

Anger is like a blazing fire fueled by the sparks of frustration, injustice, and disappointment. Just as a fire can quickly grow out of control if left unattended, anger can consume our thoughts and actions, leading to destructive outcomes. However, like a fire, anger can also be harnessed and channeled in productive ways. By learning to tend the fire of our anger with mindfulness and self-awareness, we can control its intensity and direction. We can choose to stoke the flames of positive change, using our anger as a catalyst for addressing injustices, setting boundaries, and advocating for ourselves and others. Like a well-tended fire provides warmth and illumination, controlled anger can ignite our passion, resilience, and determination to create a better world. By intentionally managing the fire within us, we can transform anger from a destructive force into a source of personal growth and positive transformation.

Remember, when anger surges within you, you have a choice. You can allow it to consume you, dictating your actions and impairing your judgment. Alternatively, you can take control of your anger, responding with thoughtfulness and compassion. Embrace the power of choice and empower yourself to navigate anger triggers with grace and resilience. By doing so, you not only cultivate personal growth but also contribute to a more harmonious and understanding world.

CONCLUSION

In conclusion, navigating anger triggers is a profound opportunity for personal growth and transformation. It is crucial to recognize that anger is a natural and valid emotion, but how we respond to it determines the course of our lives. By developing self-awareness, we gain the power to recognize our triggers, understand the underlying emotions, and choose how we express and manage our anger. This journey requires self-compassion as we learn to navigate past traumas, heal from painful experiences, and cultivate healthier coping mechanisms. Remember, your anger does not define you, but your ability to acknowledge them, seek support, and implement positive change will have the ultimate effect. By embracing this journey with courage, empathy, and a commitment to personal growth, you can transform your anger triggers into catalysts for healing, resilience, and a profound connection with yourself and others.

In exploring anger triggers, we uncover the depth of our emotions and the power of our choices. Our triggers provide valuable insights into our needs, boundaries, and unresolved wounds. By proactively facing our triggers, we embark on a journey of self discovery, healing, and self-empowerment. This journey invites us to cultivate compassion, both for ourselves and others, as we navigate the complexities of anger and its triggers. Through self-reflection, therapy, and the development of healthy coping strategies, we can break free from the cycle of reactive anger and embrace a more balanced and authentic way of being. Remember, you have the power to transform anger triggers into opportunities for growth, understanding, and the cultivation of deep empathy.

As we conclude this chapter, let us remember that our experiences are valid, and our emotions deserve acknowledgment and compassionate understanding. Through this recognition that we can embark on a path of healing, growth, and empowerment. By embracing self-awareness, seeking support, and implementing effective strategies, we can liberate ourselves from the grip of anger triggers and cultivate a life rooted in resilience, empathy, and personal fulfillment. Remember, the journey toward healing and transformation is unique for each individual. However, by sharing our insights, supporting one another, and fostering a culture of compassion, we can collectively create a world where anger triggers become instruments towards inner peace and authentic connection.

CHAPTER 2

MAKE HEALTHY
HABITS YOUR HOME

In today's ever-changing society, there exists an imbalanced abundance of unhealthy foods, detrimental media, and unfavorable activities that have a damaging effect on individuals from all backgrounds. It is crucial to recognize that what we consume greatly reflects our identity and values. The content we allow into our minds, the food we intake, and the media and information we absorb significantly influences our physical and emotional well-being. By understanding the

51

profound impact of our consumption habits, we can make more informed choices that align with our desired self-image and contribute to our overall health and happiness.

A structured lifestyle provides a solid foundation for cultivating and maintaining healthy habits. It is essential to establish and sustain routines that promote well-being that become ingrained into our lifestyle. By incorporating a sense of order and organization into our daily lives, we create an environment that encourages consistency and discipline. This structured approach allows us to prioritize and allocate time for healthy habits such as regular exercise, nutritious meals, quality sleep, and spending quality time with loved ones. A structured lifestyle makes us more likely to make intentional choices that support our physical and mental health, leading to improved overall well-being.

On the other hand, an unstructured lifestyle can have detrimental effects on overall well-being. Without a routine, individuals may struggle to manage their time efficiently, resulting in disorganized and unproductive days. Irregular sleep patterns associated with an absence of a set schedule can lead to chronic fatigue and decreased cognitive function. Also, inconsistent eating habits that lack structure and balance can negatively impact physical health and mental well-being. Unstructured lifestyles may also strain relationships as individuals become unreliable and unpredictable in their interactions. By adopting healthy habits and embracing structure, individuals can mitigate these challenges, promoting improved well-being, stronger relationships, and a higher quality of life.

AS YOU SOW, SO SHALL YOU REAP

The phrase "As you sow, so shall you reap" highlights that the quality and quantity of our outcomes depend on the quality and quantity of our inputs. This principle applies to various aspects of our lives. The food we consume, the information and media we absorb, and the habits and routines we establish all shape our future consequences. By consciously choosing healthy nutrition, seeking reliable information, and cultivating positive habits, we increase the likelihood of reaping favorable outcomes, while neglecting these areas may lead to negative repercussions.

Imagine a farmer carefully selecting high-quality seeds and planting them in nutrient-rich soil, diligently treating them carefully. As the farmer ultimately reaps a bountiful harvest from these efforts, we also can plant seeds for our future and nurture our well-being through conscious consumption. The decisions we make in the present have a lasting impact on our future, and what we consume daily plays a crucial role in shaping the person we will become. By carefully selecting high-quality "seeds" in the form of our choices, we increase our chances of reaping positive outcomes and experiencing personal growth, just as the farmer reaps a bountiful harvest.

Our choices regarding consumption play a pivotal role in shaping our identity. They reflect our values, preferences, and beliefs, influencing our self-perception and how others perceive us. Food, in particular, holds significant power in this process. The types of food we consume and our approach to eating reveal aspects of our cultural background, personal values, and level of health consciousness. By opting for nutritious food and beverages, engaging with uplifting media content, and cultivating healthy habits, we can actively contribute to positive outcomes in our lives.

To unlock our full potential, we must embrace intentional and mindful consumption. It is vital to make conscious choices about the food and drinks we consume, prioritizing high-quality options that truly nourish our bodies. Additionally, being selective about the media we engage with, opting for content that is positive and uplifting, can contribute to a more optimistic outlook. Furthermore, establishing healthy habits and routines that foster overall well-being becomes the cornerstone of our success. By sowing the seeds of intention and mindfulness, we cultivate the ideal conditions to harvest a life of extraordinary health, boundless happiness, and remarkable achievements.

Correlation of Food and Well-Being

Many people may be unaware of the direct connection between food and emotional well-being. However, scientific research has shown that our diet can influence our mood and emotional state. Consuming a balanced diet that includes a variety of nutrient-rich foods is crucial for obtaining essential vitamins and minerals. These nutrients are necessary for our bodies to function optimally, including our brain and nervous system, which significantly impact our emotional well-being. Vitamins and minerals are vital in synthesizing and regulating neurochemicals and hormones that affect our moods and emotions. For example, certain nutrients like omega-3 fatty acids, B vitamins, and magnesium are involved in producing and regulating neurotransmitters such as serotonin, dopamine, and norepinephrine, which are associated with mood regulation.

The significance of consuming a healthy diet cannot be emphasized enough, as it directly influences both our physical and mental well-being. By incorporating a variety of fruits, vegetables, whole grains, and lean proteins into our daily meals, we promote hormonal balance, strengthen our bones and muscles, boost our immune system, and enhance cognitive clarity. Extensive research has consistently demonstrated the strong correlation between our dietary choices and mental health, underscoring the importance of prioritizing nutritious options.

Conversely, studies have also shown the detrimental effects of fast foods, processed foods, and sugary beverages on our physical and mental health, contributing to depression and anxiety (Holder, 2019). Therefore, by consciously selecting wholesome foods, we not only invest in our physical well-being but also foster positive mental health and improve our overall quality of life.

Consuming foods high in sugar and salt can cause hormonal imbalances and detrimental health effects. Research has shown that a high sugar intake can lead to insulin resistance, a condition in which the body's cells become resistant to the effects of insulin. Insulin is a crucial hormone that regulates blood sugar levels (Te Morenga et al., 2015). Insulin resistance is a key risk factor for type 2 diabetes and obesity (Younossi et al., 2016). Moreover, consuming foods high in salt can also increase the risk of developing high blood pressure and cardiovascular diseases (World Health Organization, 2022). Additionally, these physical ailments can have emotional consequences such as anxiety, irritability, and depression (Beydoun & Wang, 2010).

A well-rounded diet that includes whole foods, such as fruits, vegetables, whole grains, and lean proteins, is vital for optimal health. These foods are abundant in essential nutrients that are crucial for the well-being of both the body and mind. For instance, a study conducted by the Department of Psychology at the University of Otago and published in the journal PLOS One showed that individuals who consumed more fruits and vegetables reported increased vitality and motivation compared to those who consumed fewer (Whiteman, 2017). Similarly, a study published in the Journal of Psychopharmacology demonstrated that nutrient-rich diets can enhance cognitive function and mood, reducing the risk of depression and anxiety (Rao et al., 2008). These findings highlight the significant impact of a balanced diet on overall health and mental well-being.

A healthy and balanced diet offers vital nutrients for optimal physical functioning, which lowers the risk of chronic diseases like heart disease, diabetes, and obesity. Research shows that a nutritious diet can reduce the risk of coronary heart disease by 30% (Yu et al., 2018) and lower the risk of obesity (He et al., 2004). Conversely, consuming processed and high-fat foods increases the likelihood of chronic diseases (Juul et al., 2021). By making positive dietary changes, individuals can improve their physical and mental health, boost energy levels, and enhance their overall quality of life (Harvard T. H. Chan School of Public Health, n.d.). Prioritizing a balanced and wholesome diet empowers individuals to take control of their well-being and enjoy a better life.

Importance of Food Quality

The lifestyle we lead significantly impacts the quality of the foods we consume. Maintaining a balanced lifestyle translates into a balanced diet. However, there are instances when our busy schedules and limited time make it challenging to prepare a well-rounded meal. As a result, we may opt for fast food or quick meals that are convenient but lack nutritional value compared to homemade, fresh foods. While these quick options may temporarily satisfy our hunger, they often fall short of providing the essential nutrients our bodies need. Over time, eating unhealthy food can decrease energy levels, mood swings, and other adverse health effects.

Reinforcing the proverbial wisdom "you will reap what you sow" highlights how the foods we consume ultimately become the fuel that our bodies rely on for optimal functioning. It is through a well-balanced diet that we can effectively nourish our bodies with the necessary nutrients they require to function efficiently and thrive. High-quality foods are an essential part of a healthy diet and lifestyle. These foods are rich in nutrients that fuel our bodies and support optimal functioning. High quality foods are typically fresh, minimally processed, and devoid of harmful additives and preservatives. They encompass a variety of options, such as fresh fruits and vegetables, lean proteins, whole grains, and healthy fats from sources like nuts and seeds.

Conversely, low-quality foods are often highly processed and contain empty calories, unhealthy fats, and excessive sugars. Low-quality foods include fast food, sugary beverages, processed snacks, and refined grains like white bread and pasta. While these foods may be convenient and appealing, they offer limited nutritional value and can have detrimental effects on our health in the long term. Regularly consuming low-quality foods increases the risk of obesity, heart disease, and diabetes.

A healthy, balanced diet should include a variety of whole, nutrient-dense foods low in added sugars, unhealthy fats, and sodium. It is also essential to consume a variety of foods to ensure that you are getting all the essential vitamins and minerals your body needs. To promote overall well-being, it is beneficial to incorporate the following foods into your daily diet:

- Fruits and vegetables: These are packed with vitamins, minerals, and fiber and should make up a significant portion of your daily intake. Aim for a variety of colors to get a range of nutrients.

- Whole grains: Whole grains like brown rice, quinoa, and oats are good sources of fiber, protein, and complex carbohydrates. They can help regulate blood sugar levels and provide sustained energy.

- Lean proteins: Good lean protein sources include poultry, fish, beans, and tofu. These foods provide essential amino acids for building and repairing muscles and tissues.

- Healthy fats: Foods like avocados, nuts, seeds, and olive oil provide healthy fats necessary for brain function, hormone production, and cell growth.

- Minimally processed foods: Processed foods are often high in added sugars, unhealthy fats, and sodium. Choose minimally processed foods like fresh produce, whole grains, and lean proteins as much as possible.

The Myth of Dieting

Maintaining a healthy weight can be challenging, and although diets may promise quick results, they often fail to deliver long-term effectiveness. Research indicates that highly restrictive diets can lead to weight regain over time (Mann et al., 2007). However, sustainable changes in eating habits and lifestyle are vital to achieving lasting success in weight management (Johnston et al., 2014). Merely relying on discipline is insufficient for maintaining a healthy diet. It is crucial to create an environment that supports healthy choices and develops a positive relationship with food (Provencher et al., 2003). It is essential to recognize that a healthy diet is a long-term lifestyle change rather than a short-term objective.

Sustainable weight management includes a combination of healthy eating habits and regular physical activity (Guh et al., 2009). A study has shown that forming a new habit can take up to 66 days (Lally et al., 2009). Thus, while dieting may offer short-term weight loss, sustainable changes in eating habits and lifestyle are necessary for long-term weight management success. It is vital to create a positive relationship with food, establish an environment that supports healthy choices, and understand that forming new habits takes time.

Maintaining consistency with a healthy diet can be challenging due to various personal and environmental factors. However, it is crucial to manage these circumstances for long-term health benefits effectively. While occasional deviations from dietary restrictions are acceptable, it is essential to limit such instances and plan for busy days by packing a nutritious meal. It's critical to be cautious that cheat meals don't turn into binge eating, which can hinder long-term goals. When attending social events involving food, making mindful choices aligned with dietary goals is possible. Recognizing setbacks, making adjustments, and persevering toward desired outcomes are key to developing sustainable healthy eating habits over time.

Incorporating healthy habits into your daily routine can significantly enhance your overall well-being. Whether it's establishing a consistent exercise regimen, giving priority to nutritious meals, ensuring sufficient sleep, or effectively managing stress, even small changes can yield remarkable results. By embracing these practices, not only will you experience physical improvements, but you'll also enjoy mental and emotional benefits such as enhanced mood, improved focus, and reduced anxiety. To help you maintain a healthy lifestyle and promote overall well-being, here are some valuable tips:

- Maintain a consistent eating schedule that aligns with your sleep schedule. Avoid eating late at night and focus on consuming well-balanced meals throughout the day, packed with essential nutrients.

- Foster a healthy personal life by spending quality time with loved ones, soaking in the sunlight, and engaging in constructive activities such as exercise, outdoor pursuits, meditation, or reading.

- Prioritize physical activity, aiming for at least 30 minutes of exercise or active movement at least twice weekly. Consider incorporating enjoyable activities with friends and family to stay motivated and involved.

- Opt for natural, nutrient-rich foods like fruits, vegetables, and lean protein sources. Limit your consumption of fast food and take-out meals, which are often low in nutrients.

- Stay adequately hydrated by drinking an ample amount of water. Hydration is crucial for brain function, energy levels, and effective nutrient absorption.

- Prepare and cook the majority of your meals to have better control over the types of calories you consume and to avoid the unhealthy additives commonly found in fast food.

- Ensure you get adequate sleep each night to allow for recovery and renewed energy.

- Maintaining a consistent sleep schedule is vital for optimal brain function, mood regulation, cognitive performance, and cellular repair.

Food Consumption Affecting Mental Well-Being

The connection between our dietary choices and mental well-being is profound. Our daily food intake not only affects our physical health but also significantly influences our mental and emotional state. Just as we prioritize nourishing our bodies with nutritious foods to maintain optimal physical functioning, it is equally vital to consider the impact of our dietary choices on our mental health. The foods we consume can directly impact our mood, cognitive function, and mental clarity. By understanding and recognizing the direct relationship between nutrition and mental well-being, we can make conscious and informed choices that support our mental health, leading to a greater sense of emotional balance and vitality in our lives.

Maintaining a balance of neurochemicals is crucial for overall well-being. Neurochemicals such as dopamine and serotonin play vital roles in regulating our behavior and emotions. When dopamine levels are excessively high, individuals may experience impulsive and aggressive behaviors. This means individuals may struggle to control their actions and react impulsively to situations disregarding long-term consequences. This often leads to outbursts of anger and emotional instability. On the other hand, excessive levels of serotonin can result in a frequent startle effect, increased body temperature (fever), and difficulties falling asleep (insomnia).

Conversely, low serotonin levels are associated with several adverse effects on mental health. People with low serotonin levels may experience anxiety, a persistent feeling of worry or fear, and have difficulty managing stress. Apathy, characterized by a lack of interest or motivation, is another common symptom. Depression, which includes sadness, hopelessness, and a loss of pleasure in activities, can also be linked to low serotonin levels. Low serotonin levels can also contribute to difficulties in managing anger. When serotonin levels are insufficient, individuals may experience irritability. Mood swings can become more frequent and intense, leading to unpredictable emotional shifts.

Promoting hormonal balance through a healthy diet is one approach to mitigate the potential impact of anger related problems. A healthy diet that provides the necessary vitamins and minerals can help achieve this balance and promote homeostasis (Mehri, 2020). A balanced diet that includes essential nutrients, such as vitamins B6, B12, folate, and minerals like magnesium and zinc, can support the production and regulation of neurochemicals involved in emotional well-being. While diet plays a significant role, it is not the sole factor in maintaining this balance. Additionally, engaging in stress-reducing activities, practicing relaxation techniques, and seeking professional support, such as therapy or counseling, can all contribute to managing anger-related issues effectively.

Nutritionists can recommend dietary adjustments to improve well-being, energy levels, and immune function. Being mindful of food's impact on our bodies and minds allows for positive changes and optimal health. By acknowledging the influence of diet on anger management, individuals can proactively improve their emotional well-being, enhance anger management skills, and lead healthier lifestyles.

HEALTH IMPLICATIONS OF UNCONTROLLED ANGER

Frequent expressions of anger can have profound adverse effects on both our physical and mental health. When we openly display anger, our body responds with a stress reaction, triggering the release of stress hormones such as cortisol and adrenaline. These hormones prepare our body for a "fight or flight" response, which can be beneficial in immediate dangerous situations. However, when anger is consistently expressed and not appropriately managed, prolonged exposure to stress hormones can lead to chronic ailments.

Physically, chronic stress can take a toll on our cardiovascular system, increasing the risk of high blood pressure and heart problems. The constant surge of stress hormones can cause the blood vessels to constrict and the heart rate to rise, putting extra strain on the heart. Over time, this can contribute to developing conditions like hypertension and increase the likelihood of heart attacks and strokes. Chronic stress can also affect our digestive system, possibly leading to irritable bowel syndrome (IBS) and other gastrointestinal problems. Stress can disrupt the normal functioning of the digestive tract, causing symptoms like abdominal pain, bloating, and changes in bowel movements.

In addition to the physical health consequences, ongoing stress from frequent anger expression can profoundly impact our mental well-being. High levels of stress hormones can disrupt the balance of neurotransmitters in the brain, leading to mood disorders like anxiety and depression. Persistent anger can exacerbate these conditions, creating a cycle of negative emotions and further stress. For example, someone who consistently expresses anger in public may find themselves in constant conflict with others, leading to strained relationships and social isolation. The negative feedback loop of anger and its consequences can contribute to feelings of frustration, helplessness, and loneliness, exacerbating mental health issues.

In summary, the negative consequences of frequently expressing anger on physical and mental health underscore the significance of effectively managing our emotions. To mitigate these effects, it is crucial to cultivate healthy coping strategies, seek support from trusted individuals or mental health experts, and engage in mindfulness practices. By adopting these approaches, we can decrease the harmful impact of anger on our overall well-being and achieve a more harmonious and satisfying life.

THE EFFECTS OF ALCOHOL ON ANGER

Alcohol consumption is widely accepted in many cultures and societies, but it can have significant adverse effects, both in the short term and long term. While alcohol may initially provide temporary euphoria, it is strongly associated with aggressive behavior, surpassing other psychotropic substances in this regard, as highlighted by the World Health Organization. Moreover, studies indicate a correlation between alcohol and substance abuse, as well as difficulties in managing anger (Buddy, 2021). These issues can lead to dangerous situations, not only for the individual but also for those around them. Therefore, it is crucial to examine how alcohol affects anger management and the potential consequences of its misuse.

In times of frustration and stress, some individuals may use alcohol to find solace or relaxation. However, while initially providing a temporary euphoria, alcohol often worsens the situation in the short-term and long-term. Its effects can lead individuals to abandon their inhibitions and act impulsively, disregarding the potential adverse outcomes resulting from their impaired state of mind. Alcohol misuse can increase the probability of risky behaviors, accidents, and even legal troubles. Rather than effectively addressing the underlying causes of frustration and stress, alcohol consumption exacerbates the problems, posing additional risks and complications. It is crucial to recognize the limitations of using alcohol as a coping mechanism and seek healthier alternatives to manage stress and frustration effectively.

Alcohol abuse and anger issues can have a negative correlation, with studies showing that alcohol use can increase the risk of aggressive and violent behavior. According to the National Institute on Alcohol Abuse and Alcoholism (2004), alcohol is a depressant that can slow down the central nervous system, resulting in a range of effects on the body and mind. While some immediate effects of alcohol, such as relaxation and decreased inhibitions, may seem comforting, they can also be dangerous, particularly when alcohol is consumed in large quantities.

Excessive alcohol consumption can impair judgment and inhibitions, leading individuals to act impulsively and aggressively. According to a study published in the Journal of Studies on Alcohol and Drugs, alcohol consumption can increase the intensity of negative emotions like anger by reducing a person's ability to regulate their emotional responses (Weiss et al., 2021). This highlights how individuals already feeling angry may become more irritable and agitated after consuming alcohol, increasing the risk of aggressive and violent behavior. Also, alcohol has numerous adverse effects on the brain's prefrontal cortex, which is responsible for controlling impulses and regulating emotions. As a result, alcohol consumption can impair an individual's ability to control anger and regulate other emotions effectively while impaired.

Alcohol consumption can have significant effects on dietary habits. It often promotes the consumption of high-calorie, low-nutrient foods while reducing the intake of nutrient-dense options. This imbalance can result in weight gain, malnutrition, and increased susceptibility to chronic diseases like diabetes, heart disease, and certain types of cancer. Furthermore, alcohol can interfere with sleep, which can negatively affect nutrition. Insufficient sleep can disrupt the hormones responsible for regulating appetite, leading to overeating or poor food choices. Overall, alcohol's impact on dietary habits can have far-reaching consequences for both physical health and overall wellbeing.

It is essential to understand the negative impact that alcohol can have on one's physical and mental health. Instead of turning to alcohol as a coping mechanism, there are numerous healthy alternatives to managing stress, such as exercise, meditation, or spending time with loved ones. Seeking professional help and support, such as counseling or rehabilitation programs, can effectively address alcohol abuse and anger management issues. By prioritizing one's health and seeking appropriate help, individuals can break free from the harmful cycle of alcohol abuse and lead happier, healthier lifestyles.

HARMFUL EFFECTS OF DRUG USE

Drug use has been extensively linked to detrimental effects on mental health, specifically in relation to the escalation of anger problems. When individuals consume drugs, such as stimulants, alcohol, or certain illicit substances, their brain chemistry undergoes alterations that contribute to changes in behavior and emotional regulation. These psychoactive substances have the potential to heighten impulsivity and aggression, resulting in unpredictable actions and adverse outcomes. A study published in the Journal of Substance Abuse Treatment found that individuals who use drugs are more likely to experience anger and aggression than those who do not use drugs (Laitano et al., 2022). Drug use and substance abuse can impair judgment, diminish inhibitions, and compromise the ability to manage emotions effectively, further contributing to heightened anger and aggression.

Drug use can also lead to the development of mental health disorders such as depression and anxiety, which can further exacerbate anger issues. A study published in the Journal of Addictive Diseases found that individuals with co-occurring anger issues and substance use disorders had worse outcomes in terms of treatment and overall functioning than those with substance use disorders alone (Quello et al., 2005). Some examples of harmful effects of drug use include addiction, overdose, mental health disorders, impaired judgment and decision-making, and social and economic consequences.

Drug addiction is a chronic and often relapsing brain disease that can lead to many negative consequences, including physical and psychological dependence, withdrawal symptoms, and an increased risk of overdose. Examples of drugs linked to increased anger and aggression include stimulants such as cocaine and amphetamines, as well as alcohol and opioids. These substances can alter brain chemistry and lead to increased impulsivity and aggression. According to the National Institute on Drug Abuse, approximately 10% of drug users become addicted (NIH, 2015).

Overdose is another potentially harmful effect of drug use, which can be life-threatening. An overdose occurs when an individual takes a higher drug dose than their body can handle, leading to respiratory depression, seizures, and coma. According to the Centers for Disease Control and Prevention (2022), over 93,000 people died from drug overdoses in the United States in 2020. Drug use can also lead to the development of mental health disorders, including depression, anxiety, and psychosis. A study published in the Journal of Psychiatric Research found that individuals who used cannabis had a higher risk of developing psychotic disorders than those who did not use cannabis (Hall & Degenhardt, 2008).

The consequences of drug use on mental health, personal well-being, and social functioning underscore the urgent need for effective prevention, intervention, and treatment strategies. Engaging in drug use not only jeopardizes an individual's physical health but also poses a threat to the well-being of others. Moreover, drug use has far-reaching social and economic ramifications, leading to unemployment, financial hardships, and strained relationships with family and friends. These repercussions further contribute to heightened levels of stress, frustration, and anger, exacerbating existing anger issues and giving rise to new emotional challenges.

SOLUTIONS TO DETER ALCOHOL AND DRUG USE

Effectively addressing alcohol and drug use requires a comprehensive approach that acknowledges the diverse motivations behind individuals' behavior. While some people may use substances as coping mechanisms for stress, trauma, or emotional difficulties, others might engage in recreational or experimental use without relying on substances to cope. To manage these issues, it is crucial to understand the underlying reasons for an individual's substance use and provide appropriate support and interventions accordingly. A multifaceted approach allows for a more comprehensive strategy for prevention, treatment, and support for those facing addiction and mental health challenges.

Social and environmental influences significantly shape attitudes toward substance use. Creating awareness about the impact of peer pressure, cultural norms, and social settings can help deter individuals from turning to alcohol and drugs as coping mechanisms. Encouraging positive social connections and promoting alternative outlets for stress relief can also reduce the appeal of substance use in social situations.

Mental health plays a critical role in substance use patterns. Addressing underlying mental health issues through early intervention and access to mental health services can provide healthier coping mechanisms for individuals dealing with anxiety, depression, or PTSD, reducing their reliance on substances for self-medication.

Fostering self-esteem and self-worth through positive reinforcement and building resilience can help prevent individuals from seeking validation through substance use. Encouraging individuals to find healthy sources of self-esteem and acceptance in their personal growth journey can diminish the appeal of using substances to boost confidence temporarily.

Dealing with life's challenges effectively is vital in preventing substance use as an escape. Support systems, counseling, and stress reduction techniques can empower individuals to face difficulties head-on, reducing the temptation to seek temporary relief through alcohol and drug use.

Understanding the neurobiological aspects of substance use and addiction is essential. By educating individuals about the potential for dependency and the long-term effects of substance use on brain chemistry, we can empower them to make informed decisions and avoid falling into addictive behaviors.

By combining these solutions and fostering a supportive environment, we can deter alcohol and drug use as coping mechanisms and promote healthier alternatives for managing stress, emotions, and life challenges. Recognizing the complexity of substance use allows us to create a more effective and compassionate approach to addressing addiction and supporting those in need. Listed below are effective strategies to help individuals avoid using alcohol and drugs as coping mechanisms for anger issues:

- *Develop Emotional Awareness and Regulation*: Individuals can become more aware of their emotions and identify and modify negative thought patterns and behaviors. Education on identifying triggers and understanding the underlying causes of anger can help take preventative measures rather than reliance on substance use as a coping mechanism.
- *Identify and Address Underlying Issues*: Sometimes, anger management issues stem from underlying emotional or psychological factors, such as trauma, unresolved grief, or untreated mental health conditions. Seeking professional help from a therapist or counselor can provide support and guidance to address and heal the underlying emotional or psychological factors contributing to their anger.
- *Build Healthy Coping Mechanisms*: Individuals can develop a toolbox of healthy coping mechanisms for managing anger.

Activities can include physical exercise, practicing relaxation techniques like yoga or meditation, engaging in creative outlets like art or music, journaling, or seeking social support through talking to a trusted friend or therapist.

- *Have a Supportive Network*: Individuals must surround themselves with a supportive network of friends, family, or support groups. A reliable support system provides a safe space for individuals to share their experiences, seek advice, and receive validation without turning to substances. This network can also serve as a source of accountability and encouragement to avoid using substances as a coping mechanism for anger.

- *Seek Professional Help*: Seeking help from a therapist, counselor, or support group can enhance anger management techniques and foster personal growth. Being in a supportive environment can provide valuable insight into underlying issues that may prevent dependence on substance use.

EFFECTS OF SOCIAL MEDIA AND TELEVISION ON ANGER

Social media and television play a pervasive role in modern society, with both positive and negative impacts on individuals and society. On the positive side, they offer valuable educational and entertainment opportunities, informing individuals about current events and enabling learning. Conversely, constant exposure to distressing and provocative content on social media platforms can trigger negative emotions and exacerbate anger in individuals. The portrayal of conflicts, arguments, and aggressive behavior on television shows or news programs can also fuel anger and frustration.

One significant factor in the relationship between media exposure and anger management issues is the potential for desensitization. Repeated exposure to violent or aggressive content through media can desensitize individuals to real-world violence, leading to reduced responsiveness and increased tolerance for aggressive behaviors. The desensitization caused by this exposure can distort individuals' perception of acceptable or appropriate behavior, ultimately contributing to anger issues. Extensive research has shown that exposure to violent media is associated with heightened aggression and anger, particularly in individuals predisposed to such behaviors.

Social media has become an integral part of modern life, but it also presents challenges, particularly in how people perceive it as a real place akin to offline interactions. This confusion arises from the way social media encourages individuals to engage with others virtually, blurring the lines between online and offline existence. Also, the virtual nature of these interactions can lead to misunderstandings and misinterpretations due to the absence of non-verbal cues and context. Without facial expressions, body language, or tone of voice, it becomes easier for people to misrepresent themselves or their intentions, leading to disingenuous conversations.

One of the key contributors to fueling anger issues in online interactions is the anonymity and disinhibition that social media offers. The digital environment allows individuals to detach from real-life consequences and adopt pseudonyms, making it tempting for some to express anger or hostility more freely. This anonymity can embolden users to engage in aggressive behavior, further escalating conflicts and creating hostile online environments.

Moreover, social media platforms can become echo chambers where users are surrounded by like-minded individuals, reinforcing their beliefs and opinions. When confronted with opposing viewpoints, polarizing discussions can arise, and emotions can run high, leading to heightened anger. Furthermore, spreading misinformation and fake news on social media can also trigger anger and frustration among users who feel deceived or manipulated by false information.

Beyond echo chambers and misinformation, online interactions can become toxic through cyberbullying and trolling. The veil of anonymity enables individuals to target others with hurtful or offensive messages, leading to emotional distress and exacerbating anger issues in both the victims and those engaged in such behavior.

The constant connectivity and exposure to social media can also have a detrimental impact on mental well-being. As people constantly compare their lives to others, feelings of inadequacy and jealousy can arise, contributing to anger, resentment, and dissatisfaction. The pressure to present a curated and perfect life on social media can lead to frustration and emotional turmoil, further impacting one's mental health and exacerbating anger-related issues.

It is equally important to develop a healthy relationship with social media and online platforms by regularly evaluating the result of our interactions, unfollowing or muting triggering accounts, and curating our online environment with positive and uplifting content. Setting boundaries on social media use can aid in developing healthy coping mechanisms to manage anger triggers effectively. It is important to actively seek out diverse perspectives, engage in respectful dialogue, and cultivate a balanced media diet that includes reliable sources of information. By exercising caution, critical thinking, and mindful consumption, individuals can navigate social media and television in a way that promotes personal growth, understanding, and constructive interactions.

EFFECTS OF SOCIAL MEDIA ON INTERPERSONAL RELATIONSHIPS

In today's digital age, social media has undeniably transformed the way we connect and interact with others. While it offers unprecedented opportunities for communication and networking, it has also introduced new challenges and complexities to our interpersonal relationships. On the one hand, social media has the potential to bridge geographical distances, allowing us to stay connected with friends and family across the globe. It provides a platform for sharing our lives, celebrating milestones, and expressing support. However, this constant virtual presence can also create a false sense of connection, leading to superficial interactions and diminishing the quality of face-to-face communication. The curated nature of social media profiles can foster comparison, envy, and insecurity, as we often perceive others' lives as more exciting or successful than our own. This can strain relationships and erode the authentic connections we crave.

The addictive nature of social media can monopolize our time and attention, leading to a lack of presence in real-world relationships. The constant need for validation through likes and comments can divert our focus from meaningful interactions with those physically present in our lives. The pressure to maintain an online persona and seek external validation can create a barrier to genuine connection and intimacy. The speed and brevity of online communication can also hinder the development of deep emotional bonds, as nuances and subtleties often get lost in text-based interactions. Furthermore, social media can become a breeding ground for conflicts, misunderstandings, and miscommunications, as tone and intention can easily be misinterpreted without non-verbal cues.

Imagine engaging in a heartfelt conversation with a loved one. While in person, we can observe their body language, the subtle shifts in their facial expressions, and the tone of their voice, all of which provide context and meaning to their words. However, when confined to digital communication, we lose these vital cues. It's as if we're conversing through a static image rather than being fully present. The absence of nonverbal cues robs us of a holistic understanding of the other person's emotions and intentions, leading to potential confusion and misunderstandings.

Furthermore, the chronic use of hollow symbols and simplistic expressions online can spill over into our offline interactions, much like relying on filtered images and staged poses in everyday life. When we become accustomed to presenting ourselves in a curated and superficial manner online, we risk carrying these habits into real-life situations where deeper connections and substantive dialogue are essential. For example, while photographs capture moments, they can never fully replicate the intricate details of real life. Similarly, our digital exchanges often fail to cultivate the same level of meaningful connections forged through physical contact and face-to-face interactions.

It is essential to acknowledge the limitations of digital communication and actively prioritize genuine physical contact and substantive dialogue. While social media offers benefits, we must remain mindful of its impact on our relationships. By recognizing the potential pitfalls and adopting healthy social media habits, we can preserve and nurture authentic connections. Striking a balance between our online and offline interactions, setting boundaries, and prioritizing face-to-face communication enables us to deepen our relationships and enrich their quality. Engaging in open and honest conversations becomes pivotal, allowing us to foster understanding, empathy, and compassion. Rather than succumbing to the quick judgments and snap reactions encouraged by social media, we must invest time in active listening and thoughtful dialogue to bridge gaps and forge stronger connections.

HEALTHY HABITS TO CONTROL ANGER

Achieving happiness and maintaining a healthy lifestyle can be challenging in today's fast-paced world.

However, it is crucial to prioritize self-care and strike a balance between work and leisure. By incorporating healthy habits into our daily lives, we can promote overall well-being. Such practices include regular exercise, a balanced diet, and sufficient sleep to enhance physical health and minimize the risk of chronic illnesses. Equally important is nurturing our mental health by practicing mindfulness, managing stress, and engaging in activities that bring us joy. Our physical health is interdependent with mental well-being. Cultivating habits such as expressing gratitude, fostering meaningful relationships, and prioritizing self-care can profoundly improve our emotional well-being.

Developing helpful habits can significantly improve emotional control, especially for individuals struggling with anger. By prioritizing our physical and mental wellbeing, we embark on a transformative journey to create a foundation for emotional stability and resilience. One practical approach is to set clear health goals and plan to achieve them. Establishing a routine and dedicating specific time for exercise, nourishing meals, and self-care activities is vital. To bolster our commitment, seeking an accountability partner or joining a community with shared health goals provides invaluable support and motivation. Let's recap some of the healthy habits we've explored that have the potential to enhance our overall well-being:

- *Exercising regularly*: Physical activity improves cardiovascular health, boosts mood, increases energy levels, and enhances overall quality of life. Aim for at least 5-10 hours a week of activities like jogging, swimming, or resistance training.
- *Eat a healthy diet*: Consume a diet rich in fruits, vegetables, whole grains, lean protein, and healthy fats to reduce the risk of chronic diseases. Limit processed and sugary foods, opting for complete, nutrient-dense options.
- *Get enough sleep*: Aim for seven to eight hours of quality sleep each night to enhance cognitive function, mood, and physical health. Establish a consistent sleep routine and create a sleep friendly environment.

- *Practice stress management*: Engage in stress-reducing activities like yoga, meditation, or deep breathing exercises to promote relaxation and reduce stress levels. Make these activities a regular part of your routine.
- *Maintain social connections*: Socialize with friends and family to boost mood, foster a sense of belonging, and receive support during difficult times. Stay connected through in-person gatherings, phone calls, or virtual meetups.
- *Practicing good hygiene*: Regularly wash hands, brush teeth, and shower to reduce the risk of illness and maintain overall well-being.
- *Refrain alcohol and drug use*: Excessive alcohol and drug use can negatively impact physical and mental health. It's best to avoid these substances altogether, seeking professional help for addiction or substance abuse.
- *Prioritize mental health*: Make time for activities that promote mental well-being, such as journaling, constructive hobbies, or seek therapy or counseling when needed.
- *Engage in lifelong learning*: Continuously expand your knowledge and skills through reading, attending workshops, or taking online courses to foster personal growth and intellectual stimulation.

CONCLUSION

Throughout this chapter, we have explored the interconnected relationship between diet, media, social media, and anger management. We have delved into the profound impact of our food consumption on our emotional well-being, acknowledging that what we consume can significantly influence our mood and our ability to manage anger effectively. Moreover, we have examined how media and social media platforms can trigger and amplify feelings of anger, as well as their influence on our interpersonal relationships. By gaining a deeper understanding of these connections, we have acquired valuable insights into the factors contributing to anger and have equipped ourselves with strategies to navigate these challenges more effectively.

In exploring our diet, we have highlighted the importance of nourishing our bodies with wholesome foods that support mental and emotional well-being. By being mindful of our food choices and understanding the impact of nutrients on neurochemical balance, we can take control of our anger and cultivate a greater sense of emotional balance. Similarly, our investigation into the role of media and social media has revealed the potential pitfalls of excessive consumption and its negative impact on our anger management and interpersonal relationships.

As we conclude this chapter, let us reflect on the profound influence that diet, media, and social media have on our emotions and interactions. It is essential to acknowledge that we have the power to make conscious choices in these areas, allowing us to reclaim control over our anger and foster healthier relationships. By adopting a balanced and nourishing diet, we provide our bodies and minds with the fuel they need to maintain emotional stability. Simultaneously, by adopting mindful media and social media habits, we can create a positive digital environment that supports our well-being and reduces anger triggers.

In this modern age, where our lives are deeply intertwined with technology and information consumption, it is crucial to cultivate awareness and intentionality. By practicing mindfulness in food choices, media consumption, and social media interactions, we can proactively manage our anger and enhance our overall emotional well-being. Remember that anger is a powerful emotion, but we can transform it into a constructive force that propels us toward personal growth and stronger relationships.

As you move forward, I encourage you to integrate the insights and strategies from this chapter into your daily life. Please pay attention to the foods you consume and how they make you feel. Be mindful of your media and social media habits, recognizing their potential impact on your emotions. By making conscious choices and developing healthy habits in these areas, you can create a positive foundation for managing anger and cultivating more meaningful connections. Remember, the journey toward anger management and emotional well-being is ongoing. Still, with dedication and self-awareness, you can navigate the complexities of what you consume in a way that supports your personal growth and a more fulfilling life.

CHAPTER 3

ESTABLISH VALUABLE RELATIONSHIPS

P ersonal relationships are a pivotal force in shaping our individual growth and development. Relationships act as mirrors, reflecting certain aspects of our personality, values, and interests while offering us opportunities to learn and grow. For individuals struggling with anger issues, these relationships can hold an even greater significance, as they can provide a crucial support system and offer valuable insights into managing and transforming anger. While genetics, cultural background, education, and personal choices contribute to our identity, relationships help empower us to become more of our true nature. Understanding the crucial role of relationships in the context of anger management is essential for fostering personal growth, emotional well-being, and constructive ways of navigating life's challenges.

The people we surround ourselves with can give us valuable insights, emotional support, and a sense of belonging. Positive relationships can be a source of encouragement, empowerment, and motivation, fostering self-esteem and confidence. Being surrounded by supportive and understanding individuals can create an environment where individuals feel safe to express themselves, including their anger. In such relationships, individuals dealing with anger issues may find understanding allies who can help them navigate their emotions and develop healthier coping mechanisms. Positive relationships can help reinforce constructive behavior and positive qualities, thus aiding in anger management and personal growth.

Conversely, negative relationships can detrimentally affect individuals dealing with anger issues. Toxic or unsupportive relationships can contribute to the escalation of anger and hinder personal growth. Constant conflicts, miscommunication, and unresolved relationship issues can fuel frustration, resentment, and anger. Individuals may find themselves trapped in a cycle of anger and hostility, unable to find healthy ways to manage their emotions. Negative relationships can also erode self-esteem and perpetuate negative beliefs about oneself, intensifying anger issues. It becomes crucial for individuals to assess the impact of their relationships on their emotional well-being and make necessary changes to foster healthier and more supportive connections.

THE PURPOSE OF RELATIONSHIPS

Relationships form the fabric of our lives, intricately weaving together the threads of connection, growth, and fulfillment. They provide us with a profound sense of purpose, enabling us to establish deep and meaningful connections with others as we navigate the intricacies of our existence. As social beings, humans have an innate need for relationships. Whether with family, friends, or romantic partners, these relationships are pivotal in shaping our identity, influencing our choices, and profoundly impacting our overall wellbeing. They provide a support system, a source of love and companionship, and a platform for personal growth and development. The bonds we forge with others can offer solace during difficult times, celebration during moments of joy, and a sense of belonging and acceptance.

One of the overarching purposes of relationships is to provide us with a sense of belonging and support. Through meaningful connections, we find solace in knowing that we are not alone in our triumphs and tribulations. Relationships offer a haven to share our joys, sorrows, fears, and vulnerabilities, knowing we will be met with understanding and compassion. They provide emotional security and nourish our souls, fostering resilience in the face of adversity.

Relationships are mirrors, reflecting aspects of ourselves that we may not readily see. They hold up a mirror to our strengths, weaknesses, and areas for growth, prompting self-reflection and self-discovery. Through the eyes of those we hold dear, we gain valuable insights into our own beliefs, values, and behaviors, empowering us to evolve and become the best versions of ourselves. Relationships become a catalyst for personal growth, pushing us to confront our limitations, challenge our assumptions, and embrace new perspectives.

In addition, relationships offer us a platform for learning and expansion. Each person we encounter has unique experiences, wisdom, and perspectives. By engaging in meaningful conversations, sharing stories, and exchanging ideas, we broaden our horizons and deepen our understanding of the world. Relationships become a script of diverse thoughts and perspectives, igniting our curiosity and fostering intellectual stimulation. They introduce us to new possibilities, inspire us to pursue our passions and help us uncover hidden talents and strengths.

Ultimately, the purpose of relationships lies in their transformative power. They have the capacity to uplift, heal, and inspire us. Through authentic connections, we find profound fulfillment and meaning. Relationships challenge us to become more compassionate, understanding, and empathetic. They provide us with opportunities to love and be loved, to give and receive support, and to grow together as individuals and as a collective. In a world often characterized by individualism and isolation, relationships remind us of our shared humanity and the interconnectedness that binds us all.

IMPACT OF HEALTHY RELATIONSHIPS ON CONTROLLING ANGER

Healthy relationships profoundly impact controlling anger, as they are built on the pillars of mutual interests and understanding, with reciprocity at their core. When individuals share common interests and truly comprehend each other's needs, desires, and values, a deep connection forms, fostering emotional closeness and trust. This strong bond creates a supportive environment where emotions can be expressed freely, reducing the likelihood of anger and frustration build-up. In such relationships, communication is open and spontaneous, allowing individuals to communicate their feelings and concerns without fear of judgment or rejection. This openness promotes emotional release, preventing anger from festering within and causing unnecessary conflict.

Active listening is a fundamental and vital aspect of healthy relationships when managing anger effectively. By genuinely engaging in active listening, individuals go beyond merely hearing the words spoken by the other person; they focus on understanding the emotions, concerns, and underlying feelings being conveyed. This attentive and empathetic approach enables them to gain valuable insights into the other person's emotional state, fostering a deeper connection and sense of emotional closeness. As a result, misunderstandings are less likely to occur, as individuals are more attuned to each other's perspectives and needs. This empathetic communication not only helps prevent anger-triggering misunderstandings but also promotes better emotional regulation.

Humility is a cornerstone of maintaining a balanced and harmonious relationship. When individuals practice humility, they acknowledge that they don't need to be right all the time, and they are open to considering other perspectives. This shift in mindset prevents ego-driven arguments and power struggles, which can often trigger anger and conflicts. Instead, humility fosters respect and compassion within the relationship, where each person's opinions and feelings are valued. In this empathetic environment, conflicts can be approached with understanding and a willingness to find common ground, leading to more peaceful and amicable resolutions.

Avoiding aggression is a crucial characteristic contributing to positive relationships and anger management. When individuals are mindful of their emotional responses and refrain from resorting to aggressive behavior, conflicts are less likely to escalate into heated arguments. In a relationship where aggression is kept in check, there is room for constructive communication and problem-solving. Disagreements can be approached calmly and with empathy, allowing both parties to express their concerns and feelings without fear of hostility or retaliation. This creates a safer emotional space, reducing the emotional strain that often leads to anger outbursts.

Healthy relationships also embrace accepting mistakes as opportunities for growth and learning. In these connections, individuals understand that everyone is human and prone to making errors. Rather than blaming themselves or others, they approach mistakes with a growth mindset, seeing them as chances to learn and improve. This mindset reduces self-blame and frustration, which can significantly trigger anger. By creating a culture of acceptance and learning from mistakes, individuals in positive relationships can better manage their emotions and reactions. Accepting fallibility encourages personal development and mutual support, as both partners can lean on each other during challenging times.

UNDERSTANDING THE ROLE OF RELATIONSHIPS IN ANGER MANAGEMENT

The role of relationships in anger management has the potential to shape our emotional well-being and guide us toward healthier expressions of anger. Relationships are a crucial support system, offering us the clarity to process and regulate our emotions. When we surround ourselves with individuals who genuinely care and understand our experiences, we feel validated and empowered to navigate anger more composedly. Their empathy and support create an environment where our emotions are acknowledged, helping us gain perspective and ultimately regain control over our anger.

One of the most important aspects of relationships in anger management is the power of empathy and understanding. When surrounded by individuals who genuinely empathize with our experiences and emotions, we feel seen and heard. Their ability to put themselves in our shoes and validate our feelings creates a sense of emotional safety that can diffuse our anger. By receiving empathy and understanding from others, we can better process and navigate our anger more constructively and compassionately.

Communication within relationships also plays a crucial role in anger management. Open and honest communication allows us to express our anger healthily and productively while facilitating a deeper understanding between individuals. When we engage in meaningful dialogue, we can address conflicts and triggers that may contribute to anger, find resolutions, and create a sense of harmony. Effective communication helps us express our needs, set boundaries, and find mutually beneficial solutions, ultimately fostering healthier relationships and mitigating anger triggers.

Another significant aspect is the power of emotional regulation and self-awareness. Through the reflection and feedback of our loved ones, we gain insight into our emotional patterns and triggers. This increased self-awareness allows us to recognize the early signs of anger and take proactive steps to manage it before it escalates. In the presence of supportive relationships, we can learn and practice strategies for emotional regulation, such as deep breathing, mindfulness, or seeking professional help. These tools empower us to navigate anger in a more controlled and constructive manner.

Lastly, the role of relationships extends to the realm of personal growth and transformation. When we surround ourselves with individuals who embody healthy emotional responses and coping mechanisms, we are inspired to emulate their behavior. Positive relationships provide us with role models and mentors who can guide us toward healthier ways of managing anger. They offer guidance, encouragement, and accountability, motivating us to continually work on ourselves and strive for emotional balance and wellbeing.

CHOOSING THE RIGHT FRIENDS

The freedom to choose our friends is a privilege that empowers us to shape a circle of individuals who genuinely connect with us and share our passions. Friendships are dynamic relationships that evolve and adapt alongside our personal growth and changing circumstances. They are not stagnant or fixed but somewhat fluid connections that require nurturing and mutual effort. As we navigate life's journeys, friendships have the potential to impact our lives profoundly. Therefore, it becomes imperative to choose our friends wisely and intentionally.

Choosing the right friends is essential because they influence our well-being and overall trajectory. Friends can uplift us, supporting our dreams and encouraging personal growth, or they can hinder us, holding us back from reaching our full potential. The company we keep shapes our perspectives, attitudes, beliefs, and behaviors. When we surround ourselves with individuals who share our values, aspirations, and positive energy, we create an environment that fosters mutual support, inspiration, and personal development.

The right friends not only provide emotional support and understanding but also challenge us to become better versions of ourselves. They inspire us to step out of our comfort zones, pursue our passions, and strive for excellence. In times of difficulty, they offer a shoulder to lean on, helping us navigate life's challenges with resilience and grace. They celebrate our successes genuinely and are there to provide guidance and encouragement when we stumble. Choosing friends who embody qualities such as empathy, kindness, integrity, and a growth mindset can contribute immensely to our own emotional well-being and personal growth.

Moreover, choosing the right friends enables us to create a positive and nourishing social circle. By surrounding ourselves with individuals who uplift and inspire us, we create an environment that promotes happiness, personal fulfillment, and a sense of belonging. Positive friendships foster a supportive network where we can freely express ourselves, share experiences, and receive valuable feedback. These relationships provide a space for open communication, trust, and authenticity, allowing us to cultivate deeper connections and create lasting memories.

Think of friendships like an investment, not only from a financial aspect but also from an emotional aspect. Just as financial assets can contribute to our wealth and stability, friends are valuable assets to our emotion well-being. Friends act as emotional assets, providing a supportive network that adds value to our lives. They are like stocks in a portfolio, with each friend offering unique qualities and benefits. Just as a diversified investment portfolio can mitigate risks and increase returns, a diverse group of friends can provide different perspectives, experiences, and strengths, enriching our lives in various ways.

Friendships, much like financial assets, appreciate over time as their presence in our lives becomes more meaningful and impactful. They contribute to our emotional wealth, providing comfort, joy, and a sense of belonging. Just as financial assets require careful selection and management, choosing the right friends and nurturing those relationships is crucial for our longterm happiness and success. Like any valuable asset, friends are an investment that yields immeasurable returns regarding personal growth and overall wellbeing.

By carefully selecting the right friends, we surround ourselves with an invaluable supportive network. These friends act as buffers between negative and uplifting experiences, providing balance and stability. They propel us toward our full potential by offering encouragement, inspiration, and a safe space to explore our ideas and aspirations. Having a supportive network of friends enables us to face challenges with resilience and optimism, enhancing our personal growth and wellbeing. Therefore, it is crucial to select friends that share some of these attributes that can have a positive influence on our well-being:

- *Empathy*: Empathetic friends can understand and share our feelings, providing comfort and support when we face challenges. They are compassionate listeners who validate our experiences and offer a non-judgmental space to express ourselves. Having friends who practice empathy helps us feel understood, accepted, and valued.

- *Positivity*: Positive friends radiate optimism and bring enthusiastic energy to our lives. They have a knack for finding the silver lining in difficult situations and can uplift our spirits during tough times. Being around positive friends can inspire us, increase our resilience, and encourage a more optimistic outlook.

- *Trustworthiness*: Trustworthy friends are reliable, dependable, and honest. They keep our secrets, respect our boundaries, and honor their commitments. Trust is the foundation of solid relationships, and having trustworthy friends creates a sense of safety and security. We can confide in them, knowing that our vulnerabilities are confidential and that they have our best interests at heart.

- *Supportiveness*: Supportive friends are our cheerleaders, offering encouragement, motivation, and guidance. They believe in our abilities and invest in our success. Whether offering a helping hand, providing constructive feedback, or simply being there to listen, supportive friends empower us to overcome challenges, pursue our goals, and believe in ourselves.

- *Growth-oriented*: Growth-oriented friends are driven to learn, evolve, and grow personally and encourage us to do the same. They inspire us to step out of our comfort zones, embrace new experiences, and strive for self-improvement. These friends may share similar interests or goals, and their drive for growth can ignite our motivation to pursue our passions and aspirations.

Friends Who are Negative Influences

It is important to recognize the dynamics of negative friendships and their impact on our lives. While it can be challenging to distance ourselves from these friends, it is necessary for our emotional well-being and personal growth. The dynamics of friends who are a negative influence can have a profound impact on our lives, shaping our behaviors, attitudes, and overall wellbeing. These friends may exhibit toxic traits and engage in destructive behaviors that can erode our emotional stability and hinder our personal growth.

One aspect of negative friendships is the presence of constant negativity and pessimism. These friends may consistently focus on the negative aspects of life, magnifying problems and fostering a pessimistic outlook. Their negative mindset can be contagious, gradually influencing our own perception of the world and amplifying feelings of anger, frustration, and dissatisfaction.

Another dynamic of negative friendships is the presence of manipulation and toxicity. These friends may engage in behaviors such as gaslighting, emotional manipulation, or constantly stirring up conflict. Their actions can undermine our self-esteem, create doubt and confusion, and escalate feelings of anger and resentment. The toxic atmosphere they create can be emotionally draining and impede our ability to effectively manage our anger.

Furthermore, friends who exhibit unhealthy coping mechanisms can contribute to the reinforcement of negative behaviors. For example, if a friend regularly resorts to aggression or violence as a way to deal with anger, they may inadvertently encourage and normalize such behaviors in our own lives. Being exposed to these negative coping strategies can hinder our progress in developing healthier ways to manage anger.

Additionally, negative friendships may lack empathy and understanding. These friends may dismiss or invalidate our emotions, fail to offer support during challenging times, or even criticize our attempts to address anger management issues. The absence of empathy can create a sense of isolation, erode our self-confidence, and make it more difficult to seek help or make positive changes.

Just as positive friendships are like assets, friends who are negative influences are comparable liabilities. Liabilities pose potential risks and hinder growth in business aspects. In friendships, liabilities drain our energy, discourage our aspirations, and conflict with our values, which impede our progress and well-being. Like any responsible CEO, we must carefully evaluate and manage these liabilities, making the necessary decisions to minimize their impact and seek out friendships that contribute positively to our lives.

Every person who enters our lives, whether as a friend or acquaintance, has the potential to teach us valuable lessons. Friends who serve as negative influences can provide us with a clear understanding of the qualities and behaviors we should avoid or distance ourselves from. They become living examples of what we should not want in our lives, offering us invaluable lessons on setting boundaries, recognizing toxic patterns, and prioritizing our well-being. While it may be challenging and uncomfortable to navigate such relationships, the insights gained from these experiences can contribute to our personal growth and enable us to make wiser choices in the future. Therefore, it's crucial to highlight the detrimental consequences of being associated with friends who are negative influences:

- *Enable negative behaviors*: Negative friends can enable and reinforce harmful behaviors such as substance abuse, aggression, and unhealthy coping mechanisms, making it difficult for individuals to break free from destructive patterns.

- *Emotional Drain*: Friends who are negative influences can drain our emotional energy by constantly bringing negativity, complaints, and pessimism into our lives, leaving us exhausted and overwhelmed.

- *Poor Decision-Making*: Negative friends can influence our decision-making process, leading us to engage in risky or harmful activities that we would otherwise avoid, jeopardizing our well-being and long-term goals.

- *Self-Esteem and Confidence Erosion*: Negative friends may undermine our self-esteem and confidence through constant criticism, belittlement, or comparison, eroding our self-worth and making it difficult to maintain a positive self-image.

- *Stagnation and Limited Growth*: Surrounding ourselves with negative influences can hinder our personal growth and development. Negative friends may discourage us from pursuing our dreams, trying new experiences, or taking risks, limiting our potential and keeping us complacent.

- *Increased Stress and Anxiety*: Constant exposure to negativity and drama from negative friends can lead to heightened stress and anxiety. Their presence can create a constant state of tension and unease in our lives.

HOW TO CHOOSE THE RIGHT PARTNER

When we choose the right partner, we invite into our lives someone who understands us at a deeper level and shares our values, aspirations, and vision for the future. Choosing the right partner takes on even greater significance regarding anger management. A supportive and understanding partner can play a pivotal role in helping us navigate anger with empathy, compassion, and effective communication. They become our anchor in times of emotional turbulence, offering a safe space where our anger is acknowledged and validated without judgment.

The right partner understands the complexities of anger and its underlying triggers. They possess the emotional intelligence to recognize when anger escalates and can intervene with patience and understanding. They can diffuse tense situations, helping us regain composure and find healthier ways to express our frustrations. With their support, we can develop the tools and strategies to manage our anger effectively.

It is crucial to find someone who provides emotional support, validation, and encouragement throughout life's journey. In a healthy relationship, the right partner encourages open and honest communication about anger. They create an environment where we feel safe to express emotions without fear of reprisal or invalidation. They actively listen to our concerns, validate our emotions, and work together with us to find constructive solutions. Through their understanding and patience, they help us develop healthier patterns of anger expression and management.

The right partner also serves as a role model, demonstrating healthy ways to handle anger in their actions and reactions. A partner who holds themselves accountable for their behavior and actively works on managing their own emotions will create a positive environment for growth and change. They exemplify effective communication, assertiveness, and emotional regulation, which can inspire us to adopt similar practices. Their positive influence encourages us to strive for personal growth and self-improvement in anger management.

It is important to note that the responsibility for anger management ultimately rests with us as individuals. However, having the right partner by our side can significantly enhance our ability to manage anger and cultivate a more peaceful and fulfilling relationship. Choosing the right partner requires self-reflection and self-awareness. It is crucial to be honest with oneself about relationship expectations and be open to compromise and personal growth.

Choosing the right partner is like finding a missing puzzle piece that completes your life. Like a perfect fit, a compatible partner aligns with your values and willingly grows and compromises with you. This journey takes time and effort, but when you discover that missing piece, it becomes invaluable. By choosing the right partner who embodies these attributes, we establish a partnership based on trust, understanding, and mutual growth. Here is a list of important attributes to consider when selecting the right partner:

- *Compatibility*: Look for a partner with similar values, interests, and goals. Compatibility lays the groundwork for a solid and harmonious relationship, ensuring a sense of alignment and a shared vision for the future.

- *Emotional Intelligence*: Seek a partner with emotional intelligence, which involves self-awareness, empathy, and the ability to understand and regulate emotions. A partner with emotional intelligence can effectively communicate, navigate conflicts with maturity, and create a safe and supportive emotional environment.

- *Communication Skills*: A partner with strong communication skills is essential for a healthy and thriving relationship. Effective communication involves active listening, expressing thoughts and feelings openly, and constructively resolving conflicts. Look for a partner who values open and honest dialogue and can communicate effectively in challenging situations.

- *Trust and Honesty*: Trust forms the foundation of any successful relationship. Choose a partner who demonstrates trustworthiness, honesty, and reliability. A trustworthy partner respects boundary, keeps commitments, and acts with integrity, fostering a sense of security and emotional safety.

- *Mutual Respect*: Respect is a fundamental aspect of a healthy partnership. Seek a partner who respects your opinions, boundaries, and autonomy and treats you with kindness and consideration. Mutual respect allows for individual growth and equality within the relationship.

THE ALLY ADVANTAGE

An ally and a friend are distinct relationships that serve different purposes. While both relationships are significant, they cannot interchangeably serve the same purpose. An ally is an individual who shares a common goal or interest with you and actively collaborates in achieving it. Together, allies work towards progressing on a specific cause or project, often establishing a more formal and defined relationship. The primary emphasis lies on the shared objective and the joint efforts made rather than on the personal connection between the individuals involved.

Having an ally can be immensely beneficial for personal growth and development. An ally can come in various forms, such as an associate, a support group, a coach, or a therapist. Allies provide support, guidance, and constructive feedback, helping us identify our weaknesses, challenge our assumptions, and broaden our perspectives. By building a relationship with an ally, we gain a better understanding of ourselves and our place in the world while becoming more aware of how our thoughts and actions impact others. Additionally, having an ally can help us build resilience and confidence, knowing we have someone committed to our growth and success.

The connections we have in our network play a significant role in determining our value and potential impact. Having allies can provide numerous benefits in both personal and professional contexts. When working towards a shared goal, individuals can leverage each other's strengths and skills, leading to more successful outcomes. By collaborating with allies, we can amplify our abilities, expand our reach, and achieve tremendous success. Building a solid network of partners allows us to tap into diverse perspectives, resources, and opportunities, ultimately increasing our overall value and potential. Listed are some key benefits of developing a relationship with an ally:

- *Career Advancement*: An ally within your organization can provide guidance and mentorship, advocate for advancement, and help you navigate career politics. They can offer insights into opportunities for growth, provide introductions to influential individuals, and support your professional development.

- *Skill Development*: An ally with similar interests or expertise can help you improve your skills and knowledge. They can offer advice, resources, and constructive feedback to help you enhance your abilities. Whether learning a new programming language, improving your public speaking skills, or honing your leadership abilities, having an ally by your side can accelerate your progress.

- *Emotional Support*: Allies can provide valuable support in personal and professional challenges. They can lend a listening ear, offer encouragement, and give a different perspective on difficult situations. During stress or uncertainty, having someone who understands your goals and supports your journey can significantly improve your ability to cope and persevere.

- *Networking Opportunities*: Allies often have their networks, and through these connections, they can introduce you to new opportunities and expand your reach. They may recommend you for projects, collaborations, or job openings, increasing your visibility and access to valuable resources. Building relationships with allies can open doors and create new avenues for growth and success.

- *Accountability and Motivation*: Allies can help keep you accountable for your goals and aspirations. By regularly checking in, setting milestones, and providing feedback, they can help you stay on track and motivated. The shared commitment to a common objective creates a sense of responsibility and mutual support, driving you to strive for excellence and overcome obstacles.

- *Diverse Perspectives*: Allies often bring different experiences, backgrounds, and perspectives. Engaging with people who have diverse viewpoints can broaden your understanding, challenge your assumptions, and foster creativity and innovation. By collaborating with allies who offer different perspectives, you can develop more well-rounded solutions and make better-informed decisions.

- *Increased Confidence*: Knowing that you have someone in your corner, supporting and believing in you, can boost your confidence. Having an ally who acknowledges your strengths, celebrates your achievements, and provides constructive feedback can help you build self-assurance. With this increased confidence, you are more likely to take risks, pursue challenging opportunities, and achieve success.

THE INESCAPABLE TIES OF FAMILY

Family ties are inescapable and profoundly influential, shaping our existence with a diverse range of connections. From open communication to shared responsibilities, these bonds create a nurturing environment where family members can grow and thrive. The influence of family remains constant throughout life, leaving a lasting impact on our identity, values, and sense of belonging. The significance of effective communication, affirmation, trust, shared responsibilities, and respect for privacy forges unbreakable connections that resonate throughout our lives.

Effective communication forms the cornerstone of healthy family relationships. Open and honest dialogues allow family members to express their feelings, thoughts, and concerns in a safe space. Active listening, where individuals genuinely hear and understand each other, nurtures empathy and compassion. By engaging in these practices, family members can better comprehend each other's needs and emotions, reducing misunderstandings and conflicts. This open communication fosters a supportive environment where family members feel heard and valued, strengthening the emotional bonds that tie them together.

In a healthy family, members actively affirm and support each other's aspirations and achievements. By providing positive reinforcement and emotional encouragement, they create a nurturing atmosphere that bolsters individual growth and self-confidence. Celebrating each other's successes and offering support during challenges further solidifies family bonds. This mutual encouragement fosters a sense of belonging, where family members know they can turn to each other for love and validation, cultivating resilience and enhancing overall well-being.

Trust is the bedrock of strong family relationships. It evolves through consistent honesty, reliability, and support. Family members who trust one another feel safe and secure, knowing they can rely on each other during good and challenging times. Building this sense of trust requires transparency, integrity, and keeping commitments, as it establishes a reliable foundation for all interactions within the family. Trust engenders emotional intimacy, allowing family members to share their vulnerabilities, dreams, and fears, fostering deeper connections and understanding.

In a healthy family, all members contribute to shared responsibilities and collaborate in household tasks and decisions. Encouraging active involvement from each family member fosters a sense of unity and shared commitment. By working together to fulfill family duties, they cultivate a supportive and cohesive environment. This shared responsibility teaches important life skills, instilling a sense of responsibility and accountability in each individual while reinforcing the value of teamwork and cooperation.

Respecting each other's privacy is essential for maintaining trust and boundaries within a family. It involves acknowledging and honoring personal space and individual boundaries. By recognizing the need for privacy, family members demonstrate consideration and empathy for one another's feelings and personal lives. Respecting privacy fosters a sense of autonomy and independence, promoting healthier relationships built on mutual respect and understanding.

While we can't choose our family members, we can influence how we interact with them. Establishing healthy boundaries, effective communication, and finding common ground can help strengthen our connections. It is essential to focus on the positive aspects of our relationships with family and actively work to reinforce those bonds. Family members play a vital role in our lives, and by navigating difficulties and celebrating successes together, we can develop deep and meaningful relationships. By practicing active listening, acceptance of differences, empathy, forgiveness, and dedicating quality time together, we can manage these relationships effectively. By incorporating these strategies into our interactions, we can nurture and develop more robust, fulfilling relationships with our family members:

- *Practice active listening*: Listen to your family members when they speak, giving them your full attention. Avoid interrupting and genuinely try to understand their perspectives and emotions.
- *Accept differences*: Embrace that each family member is unique, with their own beliefs, values, and opinions. Respect and acknowledge these differences without judgment or criticism.

- *Show empathy*: Put yourself in your family members' shoes and try understanding their feelings and experiences. Validate their emotions and offer support, showing that you care and are willing to empathize with their challenges.

- *Practice forgiveness*: Let go of past grievances and resentments and be open to forgiving family members for their mistakes. Holding onto grudges only creates tension and hinders the growth of relationships.

- *Dedicate quality time*: Make a conscious effort to spend meaningful time with your family. Engage in activities like shared hobbies, meals, outings, or meaningful conversations. This dedicated time helps build bonds and creates lasting memories.

CONCLUSION

As we conclude, the insights presented in this chapter underscore the profound significance of nurturing meaningful relationships in our lives. Relationships, whether they be with friends, partners, or family members, have the power to shape our personal growth, emotional well-being, and overall success.

By selecting and cultivating relationships based on shared values, mutual respect, and open communication, we create a fertile ground for personal development. Meaningful connections offer a supportive network that encourages us to explore our passions, overcome challenges, and realize our true potential. These relationships provide a safe space for self-expression, vulnerability, and growth, allowing us to navigate the complexities of life with greater resilience and grace.

Furthermore, our relationships play a pivotal role in our emotional stability. The understanding, empathy, and validation we receive from our loved ones provide us with the necessary tools to manage our emotions effectively. Through healthy and supportive relationships, we gain insight into our triggers, develop more beneficial coping mechanisms, and learn to express our emotions constructively. This, in turn, helps us navigate anger management with greater composure and self-control.

The impact of nurturing meaningful relationships extends beyond our personal lives to our overall success. Positive and uplifting relationships inspire us, challenge us, and push us to reach new heights. They serve as a source of motivation, accountability, and inspiration, propelling us toward our goals and aspirations. Surrounding ourselves with individuals who believe in our potential and encourage our growth can unlock doors of opportunity, expand our horizons, and contribute to our professional success.

As we continue to cultivate meaningful relationships, let us remember the impact of choosing our connections wisely. In essence, the quality of our relationships determines the quality of our lives. The bonds we forge today have the potential to shape our future in remarkable ways. Its imperative to approach each relationship with intentionality, authenticity, and a commitment to growth, so that we can develop relationships that enrich our lives on multiple levels.

CHAPTER 4

THE POWER OF A POSITIVE MINDSET

In the vast landscape of our minds lies a force so powerful and transformative that it has the ability to shape our experiences, shape our perceptions, and ultimately shape our lives. The way our mind functions affects every facet of our existence, from our relationships to our professional endeavors and even to our journey of anger management. A positive mindset can transform our lives in extraordinary ways. A positive attitude involves consciously directing our focus towards uplifting thoughts and beliefs, such as optimism, gratitude, and self-compassion. It requires the deliberate choice to see the good in every situation, even during challenging times. By shifting our mindset and adopting a solution-oriented approach, we can develop the resilience and optimism to navigate life's trials with strength and determination.

The mind is our most powerful resource and has the potential to unlock a world of limitless opportunities. Imagine a world where negativity, self-doubt, and pessimism are replaced with optimism, self-belief, and resilience. A world where challenges are seen as opportunities for growth, setbacks are viewed as necessary tools, and failures are embraced as valuable lessons. This is the power of a positive mindset, an inner compass that guides us through the storms of life and illuminates the path toward happiness, fulfillment, and inner peace.

Cultivating a positive mindset goes beyond momentary optimism; it is a continuous journey of reshaping our thoughts and embracing our boundless potential. Often, we find ourselves dwelling on past failures, heartbreaks, and setbacks, allowing them to overshadow the moments of happiness and peace. However, developing a positive mindset demands an ongoing commitment to reframing our thoughts, shifting our perspective, and nurturing self-awareness. It requires discipline, perseverance, and a willingness to challenge ingrained thinking patterns that may hinder our growth. With this understanding, we open ourselves to a world of possibilities and unlock the true power within us.

Through scientific research, personal anecdotes, and practical strategies, we explore the profound influence of a positive mindset on anger management. We uncover how our thoughts, beliefs, and attitudes can escalate or defuse anger and how a positive mindset can become an invaluable tool in our quest for emotional well-being. Let us embrace the power of a positive mindset and unleash our true potential as we navigate the intricacies of life.

THE SCIENCE BEHIND A POSITIVE MINDSET

When we delve into the neuroscience of positivity, we uncover fascinating insights into its profound impact on our brain and overall well-being. Research has revealed that positive emotions, such as joy, gratitude, and love, activate specific regions of the brain associated with happiness and reward. The prefrontal cortex, a key area responsible for higher-order cognitive functions, lights up with activity, facilitating rational thinking, decision-making, and problem-solving. Simultaneously, the limbic system, which governs our emotions, is vital in regulating our emotional responses and establishing a sense of well-being.

The power of a positive mindset goes beyond momentary brain activity. Studies have shown that cultivating a positive mindset can lead to structural and functional changes in the brain. Through a process called neural plasticity, our brain's neural connections are strengthened, rewired, and even created anew. This means that by consistently practicing positive thinking, we have the ability to rewire our brain's circuitry, allowing us to experience greater emotional well-being, resilience, and overall psychological health.

Positive thinking and emotional well-being go hand in hand. Our thoughts profoundly impact our emotions and adopting a positive mindset can significantly influence our emotional state. When we engage in positive thinking, we shift our focus towards the positive aspects of our lives, which enhances our overall mood and emotional well-being. Positive thinking helps us develop resilience in the face of challenges, reduces stress levels, and fosters a sense of optimism and hope. It allows us to approach situations with a more balanced and constructive perspective, leading to healthier emotional responses and better anger management.

Cultivating a positive mindset yields various psychological benefits beyond our emotional wellbeing. Research has shown that individuals with a positive mindset experience higher life satisfaction, better physical health, and improved interpersonal relationships. A positive mindset enhances our problem-solving abilities, creativity, and resilience, enabling us to navigate life's challenges more effectively. It also promotes a sense of self-efficacy and empowers us to take control of our emotions and behaviors. Ultimately, a positive mindset fosters a growth-oriented attitude, encouraging continuous learning, personal growth, and adaptability.

ELEVATING YOUR MINDSET

Elevating your mindset is the conscious effort to cultivate and nurture a positive and empowered mental state. It involves shifting your perspective, beliefs, and attitudes towards one that is more growth-oriented, resilient, and optimistic. Developing self-awareness is an essential first step on this path. Take time to reflect on your thoughts, emotions, and belief systems. Identify any negative or self-limiting patterns that may be holding you back. Once you become aware of these patterns, consciously challenge them and replace them with empowering thoughts and beliefs. Embrace affirmations and positive self-talk to rewire your mindset and reinforce optimistic perspectives.

For instance, consistently telling yourself that you are not good enough or capable enough limits your potential for success. However, by becoming aware of these negative patterns, you can actively challenge and replace them with more positive and empowering beliefs. By substituting phrases like "I can't" with "I will," you transform your mindset toward a more positive and productive outlook. This shift requires consistent practice and repetition, as well as a willingness to confront and reevaluate your thoughts and beliefs. Over time, these deliberate efforts will lead to significant personal growth, and you will begin to think differently about all aspects of your life.

Surrounding yourself with positive influences is another integral way to elevate your mindset. Seek out individuals who inspire and uplift you. Surround yourself with supportive friends, mentors, or role models who encourage your growth and believe in your potential. Engage in communities or groups that share your passions and values, providing a nurturing environment for personal development. By immersing yourself in positive and uplifting environments, you create a strong foundation for a positive mindset.

Continual learning and personal growth are key factors in elevating your mindset. Be open to new experiences, challenges, and opportunities for self-improvement. Engage in activities that expand your knowledge, skills, and perspectives. Read books, listen to podcasts, attend workshops, or enroll in courses that align with your interests and goals. By actively seeking growth and learning, you cultivate a growth mindset that fuels personal transformation and propels you forward.

Embrace failures as valuable learning experiences on your journey to elevating your mindset. Rather than letting setbacks discourage you, see them as opportunities for growth and resilience. Learn from your mistakes, extract valuable lessons, and use them as lessons for success. Adopt a mindset of curiosity and perseverance, viewing challenges as opportunities for personal and professional development.

Finally, practice gratitude and mindfulness as daily habits to elevate your mindset. Cultivate a sense of appreciation for the present moment and the blessings in your life. Regularly express gratitude for the things you have, your experiences, and the people who have supported you. Engage in mindfulness practices such as meditation, deep breathing exercises, or journaling to cultivate a calm and centered state of mind. By nurturing a grateful and present mindset, you invite positivity and contentment into your life.

The mind's power to influence physical health and wellbeing is truly remarkable. Extensive research has shown the profound connection between our thoughts, emotions, and bodily functions. Our mental state can significantly impact our immune system, cardiovascular health, and lifespan. Negative emotions and prolonged stress weaken the immune system and make us more susceptible to illnesses. In contrast, positive emotions and a positive mindset can enhance overall health and well-being. Recognizing and utilizing this mind-body connection allows us to prioritize our mental and emotional health as crucial components of our overall well-being.

Another fascinating aspect of the mind is the phenomenon known as the self-fulfilling prophecy. This concept suggests that our beliefs and expectations about ourselves and the world can shape our reality. For instance, if we hold a belief that we are not capable of achieving a specific goal, we may not even attempt to pursue it, thereby increasing the likelihood of failure. Conversely, if we believe in our ability to achieve the same goal through hard work and determination, we are more inclined to succeed.

DEVELOPING A GROWTH MINDSET

A growth mindset is a powerful belief system that recognizes the potential for growth, improvement, and learning in every aspect of life. This mindset embraces challenges, sees failures as opportunities for growth, and believes that with effort and perseverance, abilities and skills can be developed. Individuals with a growth mindset understand that intelligence and talent are not fixed traits but can be nurtured and expanded through dedication and a willingness to learn. A growth mindset empowers individuals to continually seek improvement, embrace feedback, and embrace a lifelong journey of knowledge and self-discovery.

Developing a growth mindset involves embracing failure as a valuable part of the learning process. Instead of feeling ashamed or discouraged by failures, it is essential to view them as opportunities for growth and improvement. Failure provides us with feedback and insights into our strengths, weaknesses, and areas for improvement. It allows us to analyze what went wrong and why, enabling us to adjust our strategies and approaches for better results in the future. Failure is a universal experience that everyone encounters in various aspects of life, and it is through these setbacks that we can learn valuable lessons.

Furthermore, a growth mindset can be nurtured through a commitment to lifelong learning. This entails seeking new knowledge, developing new skills, and embracing new experiences that challenge and stretch our abilities. This is achieved by seeking out opportunities to broaden our intellectual horizons and staying curious about the world around us. Whether learning a new language, mastering a musical instrument, or developing technical expertise, skill development challenges us and opens doors to new opportunities. By adopting a curious and open-minded approach, we foster a mindset that thrives on continuous learning and personal evolution.

Adopting a growth mindset in anger management brings about significant advantages. Rather than feeling helpless and defeated when we struggle to control our emotions, a growth mindset allows us to perceive anger episodes as opportunities for personal growth. Through self-reflection and analyzing the triggers that lead to our anger, we gain a deeper understanding of our emotional patterns. A heightened self-awareness empowers us to seek healthier and more effective strategies for managing our anger. By continuously learning from our experiences, we develop valuable insights and refine our coping mechanisms, thereby enhancing our ability to navigate anger constructively. Ultimately, a growth mindset enables us to transform moments of anger into a catalyst for motivation.

USING LOGIC TO MANAGE EMOTIONS

Using logic rather than relying solely on our emotions can have profound implications on our well-being and the outcomes of challenging situations. When our emotions dictate our responses to anger, we may succumb to impulsive reactions driven by frustration, resentment, or even rage. These instinctual responses can lead to many negative consequences, damaging relationships, causing regrettable actions, and further escalating conflicts.

On the other hand, employing logic to manage anger involves a deliberate and thoughtful approach. One key aspect is the ability to resist natural impulses. Controlling impulses empowers us to prioritize logical reasoning over emotional reactions. When we resist impulsive urges, we can take a step back, assess situations objectively, and make informed decisions based on rationality and long-term consequences. This self-discipline enables us to approach challenges with a clear mind, fostering better problem-solving skills and more balanced perspectives in various aspects of life.

Using logic to manage anger brings several key benefits. First, it enables us to gain control over our emotions, preventing them from overpowering our judgment and guiding us toward destructive behaviors. Instead of allowing anger to cloud our thinking, logical reasoning helps us maintain composure and consider alternative courses of action. This empowers us to respond constructively, respectfully and focused on finding solutions.

Furthermore, logic allows us to navigate complex emotional situations more effectively. It will enable us to understand the underlying causes of our anger, identify triggers, and recognize patterns in our emotional responses. By analyzing these factors, we can develop strategies to address and manage our anger in healthier ways. This may involve assertive communication, setting boundaries, seeking support, or engaging in self-care practices that promote emotional well-being.

The potential outcomes of using logic to manage anger is far-reaching. It enhances our interpersonal relationships by fostering open and honest communication, as well as promoting understanding and empathy. By approaching anger with logic, we can resolve conflicts more peacefully and effectively, fostering harmonious connections with others. Additionally, it contributes to our personal growth and self-awareness as we learn to regulate our emotions and cultivate emotional intelligence.

APPLYING A POSITIVE MINDSET TO ANGER MANAGEMENT

Applying a positive mindset to anger management can be a transformative approach that empowers us to navigate challenging emotions with grace, compassion, and resilience. By adopting a positive mindset, we shift our focus from dwelling on anger and its adverse effects to seeking constructive solutions and personal growth. This shift in perspective allows us to view anger as an opportunity for self-reflection, understanding, and positive change.

The first step in applying a positive mindset to anger management is cultivating self-awareness. This involves developing a deep understanding of our triggers, patterns of reaction, and the underlying emotions that fuel our anger. By becoming aware of these internal dynamics, we can interrupt the automatic response of anger and create space for more constructive choices.

The next step is to challenge and reframe our thoughts. We often get caught up in negative thought patterns when anger arises, reinforcing our feelings of righteousness or victimhood. By consciously questioning and reframing our thoughts, we can adopt a more balanced and rational perspective. This allows us to respond to anger with empathy, understanding, and a commitment to finding solutions rather than getting stuck in a cycle of blame and resentment.

Another critical step is practicing empathy and seeking to understand the perspectives of others. Anger often arises from unmet needs, misunderstandings, or differing viewpoints. By genuinely listening to others, empathizing with their experiences, and seeking common ground, we can foster understanding and diffuse anger. This shift in perspective not only promotes healthier communication but also strengthens relationships and fosters a sense of connection.

A crucial element of a positive mindset in anger management is the belief in our ability to change and grow. We understand that anger is a natural emotion, but it doesn't define us. By fostering a growth mindset, we embrace the notion that we can learn from our anger, develop healthier coping mechanisms, and improve our emotional well-being.

In addition, developing emotional intelligence is essential in applying a positive mindset to anger management. This involves recognizing and managing our own emotions, as well as being attuned to the feelings of others. By cultivating emotional intelligence, we can respond to anger with patience, kindness, and assertiveness rather than reacting impulsively or aggressively. This creates an environment of mutual respect and encourages productive problem-solving.

Lastly, practicing self-care is crucial in maintaining a positive mindset in anger management. Anger can be draining and emotionally taxing, so it is important to prioritize self-care activities that promote relaxation, stress reduction, and overall well-being. Engaging in activities such as exercise, mindfulness, journaling, or seeking support from trusted friends or professionals can help us recharge and approach anger with a clear and calm mindset.

OVERCOMING NEGATIVITY BIAS

Negativity bias is a natural inclination of the human brain to focus more on negative experiences and thoughts, which contributes to shaping our perceptions and responses. Negativity bias, as evidenced by various studies, manifests in several ways. Naturally, our brains respond more intensely to negative stimuli, leading to heightened reactions and potential anger outbursts. Additionally, the predominance of negative news coverage further reinforces this bias, capturing our attention and potentially fueling anger. Furthermore, the tendency to dwell on adverse events can perpetuate and amplify anger issues, as negative emotions tend to linger and receive more cognitive focus. These examples highlight how negativity bias can exacerbate feelings of anger, making it more challenging to regulate emotions effectively.

Negative thoughts can contribute to anger by triggering the release of stress hormones like cortisol and adrenaline in the brain, which activate the fight-or-flight response. This leads to physical symptoms such as increased heart rate, rapid breathing, and heightened muscle tension. This physiological response can intensify reactions to situations, leading to angry outbursts or harmful behaviors, exacerbating anger issues. By consciously reframing problems with a more balanced perspective, we can prevent anger from escalating.

One way to counteract negativity bias is through conscious awareness and intentional reframing of negative experiences. By being mindful of our automatic negative reactions, we can question their validity and actively seek alternative interpretations. This involves examining the evidence and considering different perspectives to challenge our initial negative thoughts. By consciously reframing situations in a more balanced and realistic light, we can reduce the influence of negativity bias and adopt a more positive mindset.

Negativity bias significantly impacts our relationships with friends, family, and partners in various ways. It can lead us to harbor pessimistic assumptions and expect the worst outcomes from people, shaping our initial interactions. We can counteract this bias by surrounding ourselves with positive influences and seeking social support. Engaging with supportive individuals who embody a positive mindset can help us challenge and reframe negative thinking patterns. By building a network of positive relationships, we create an environment that supports and reinforces a more optimistic perspective.

Practicing gratitude is another powerful strategy to counteract negativity bias. By deliberately focusing on the things we are grateful for, we shift our attention toward the positive aspects of our lives. This practice helps to retrain our brains to notice and appreciate the good, counterbalancing the natural inclination towards negativity. Regularly expressing gratitude, either through journaling or verbally, can cultivate a more optimistic outlook and reduce the impact of negativity bias on our emotions.

TRANSFORMING ANGER INTO MOTIVATION

Anger, typically perceived as a negative emotion, has long been associated with destructive behavior and undesirable consequences. Society often encourages us to avoid or suppress anger, emphasizing the importance of remaining calm and composed. However, an alternative perspective exists—one that recognizes anger's potential to be transformed into a constructive force capable of fueling motivation and driving positive change. When channeled appropriately, anger can serve as a catalyst for personal growth, social progress, and the pursuit of justice.

Harnessing anger as a motivational force can be a powerful tool in achieving success and reaching our goals. Imagine someone doubting your capabilities or focusing on your past failures suggesting you can't complete your goals. Instead of letting doubt consume you, allow the fire of anger to ignite within. Feel the intensity of your anger, knowing that you possess the potential and a burning desire to prove them wrong. Use that anger as a driving force to fuel your determination, propelling you forward on the path toward your aspirations. Let anger constantly remind you of your worth and abilities, pushing you to surpass expectations and showcase your true potential. As you channel your anger towards your goals, you'll discover an unwavering commitment to success, overcoming obstacles with persistent resolve while proving to yourself and others that you can accomplish any goal you pursue.

When channeled constructively, anger has the potential to drive positive changes both for ourselves and society at large. Instead of allowing anger to spiral into destructive behaviors, we can use it as a powerful catalyst for advocating positive transformations. By channeling anger into constructive actions like supporting causes, promoting dialogue, or initiating community projects, we can make a tangible impact on society. Productive means of anger can foster empathy and understanding, motivating us to seek peaceful resolutions and bridge community divides. When wielded with mindfulness and purpose, anger becomes a force for positive change, empowering us to stand up for what we believe in, make a difference in the world, and cultivate a more compassionate and just society.

Anger often arises from a sense of injustice or wrongdoing, serving as a powerful motivator for taking action and effecting positive changes in our lives. It propels us to address the underlying issues, seek resolution, and create a better future. Of course, it is crucial to note that anger should never be used as a destructive force. Transforming anger into motivation requires balance and self-control, the ability to channel our emotions positively for the greater good. Let's evaluate ways in which we can transform anger into motivation to improve our mindset:

- *Practice Self-Awareness*: Cultivate an understanding of your anger triggers and how anger manifests in your thoughts, emotions, and behaviors. By recognizing and acknowledging your anger, you can take proactive steps toward transforming it into positive motivation.

- *Reframe Anger as a Catalyst*: Shift your perspective on anger and view it as a powerful catalyst for positive change. Rather than allowing anger to consume you, channel its energy towards setting goals, seeking solutions, and taking action to address the underlying issues.

- *Take Constructive Action*: Instead of dwelling on anger or engaging in destructive behaviors, channel your energy into constructive action. Use your anger as a driving force to advocate for change, speak up against injustice, or actively work towards resolving the underlying issues.

- *Cultivate Empowerment and Gratitude*: Shift your focus from anger towards empowerment and gratitude. Recognize your strengths, achievements, and the progress you have made, while also expressing gratitude for the positive aspects of your life. This mindset shift can help you approach challenges with a more optimistic and motivated outlook.

- *Practice Self-Reflection and Continuous Improvement*: Regularly reflect on your anger experiences, evaluating how you have transformed anger into motivation and identifying areas for further improvement. Embrace a growth mindset, committing to ongoing self-reflection and personal development.

CONCLUSION

As we conclude this chapter, it is essential to recognize that cultivating a positive mindset is the key to unlocking both extraordinary success and unbridled happiness in life. By consciously elevating our mindset, adopting a growth-oriented perspective, and prioritizing logical thinking over emotional reactions, we can overcome seemingly insurmountable obstacles and reach our goals. Moreover, transforming anger into motivation offers a powerful tool to leverage our emotions constructively.

We must also acknowledge that developing and maintaining a positive mindset is a continuous journey rather than a final destination. It requires ongoing effort, self-reflection, and a commitment to personal growth. By challenging limiting beliefs, reframing negative self-talk, and embracing our anger as fuel for change, we can propel ourselves toward a happier and more fulfilling life.

So, take a moment to reflect on your mindset. Are you holding yourself back with self-imposed limitations or negative thoughts? Dare to challenge those beliefs and reshape your thinking patterns. Allow your anger to be a driving force, propelling you towards action and progress. With a positive mindset, you become a force of nature, like a mighty hurricane gathering strength, tearing through obstacles, and leaving a trail of transformative power in your wake. With your positive mindset, you become a catalyst for inspiration and empower others to unlock their hidden potential, joining you in the unstoppable wave of positive change.

With a positive mindset, you hold the key to unlocking the hidden potential within you, unleashing a force that can propel you beyond the boundaries of your wildest dreams. Embrace the belief that you deserve to live your best life, filled with joy, fulfillment, and success. Commit to nurturing and cultivating a positive mind that uplifts and empowers you in every aspect of your journey. Now is the time to embark on this transformative path, and with your newfound mindset, the possibilities are endless. Believe in yourself, harness your emotions, and let your positive mindset be the driving force that propels you toward the life you desire.

CHAPTER 5

MANAGING ANGER IN PUBLIC SITUATIONS

In a world filled with chaos and stress, navigating public spaces can often be overwhelming, especially for those dealing with anger management. Public spaces are dynamic and filled with diverse individuals, each with their own beliefs, values, and behaviors. Inevitably, conflicts and disagreements can arise, triggering intense emotions and testing our ability to regulate emotions effectively. We must not only recognize these public stressors but also equip ourselves with practical strategies to manage anger when confronted with adversity in public settings. By doing so, we can prevent detrimental outcomes, such as strained relationships, job loss, or even legal repercussions.

Managing anger in public situations requires a unique set of skills and strategies that allow us to express ourselves assertively, resolve conflicts peacefully, and maintain composure in the face of provocation. It entails understanding the triggers and underlying causes of our anger, developing effective communication techniques, and learning to navigate the complex dynamics of public environments. By approaching situations with a composed mindset, we can diffuse potential altercations in public.

Ultimately, managing anger in public situations is a skill that requires practice and patience. By combining self-awareness, emotional regulation, and effective communication, individuals can navigate public spaces with greater resilience. Through continued self-reflection, learning from past experiences, and seeking support when necessary, individuals can develop the tools to manage anger effectively and maintain healthier relationships with others in public settings.

HARMFUL EFFECTS OF ANGER IN PUBLIC

When anger is left unmanaged in public situations, it can have detrimental consequences for ourselves and those around us. Everyday stresses and triggers can cause intense emotional reactions that are difficult to control. Uncontrolled anger can lead to a range of negative consequences in public that can escalate conflicts, strain relationships, and contribute to a hostile social climate. Studies have revealed that observing expressions of anger in public settings can lead to increased aggression and negative emotions in others, perpetuating a cycle of hostility.

Anger is a highly contagious emotion that can rapidly spread from one individual to another, leading to various negative consequences. Anger in public settings can create a hostile and unpleasant atmosphere for everyone involved. Witnessing or being subjected to angry outbursts can induce fear, anxiety, and discomfort in others. Also, observing anger in others can serve as a model for imitation, encouraging individuals to respond with their anger, which further exacerbates the situation and complicates resolution efforts. It can erode trust, diminish empathy, and create a hostile social environment where people feel unsafe or uneasy.

Publicly expressing anger can have detrimental effects on our reputation and credibility. When anger is frequently displayed, trust and respect from others can diminish significantly, leading to strained personal and professional relationships. People may hesitate to offer assistance or support, fearing their actions might provoke further anger. It is crucial to recognize the impact our behavior has on those around us and take proactive steps to cultivate a more peaceful and harmonious environment.

Public displays of uncontrolled anger can have legal repercussions. If the anger escalates into aggressive or violent behavior, it may lead to confrontations with law enforcement. In some jurisdictions, aggressive outbursts in public spaces may be considered disorderly conduct or disturbance of the peace, leading to potential charges and legal penalties. Being involved in legal trouble can have severe consequences for one's personal and professional life, including possible fines, probation, or incarceration.

It's crucial to understand that managing emotions, including anger, is essential not only for our overall well-being but also for maintaining a positive and safe social environment. Seeking healthy outlets for expressing feelings and learning effective coping strategies can significantly reduce the negative impact of anger on ourselves and those around us. If someone finds it challenging to control their anger, seeking support from friends, family, or professional counseling can be beneficial in developing healthier emotional responses.

WORKPLACE STRESSORS

In the demanding environment of the workplace, stressors can have a profound impact on individuals striving to maintain control over their anger. Heavy workloads, tight deadlines, and high expectations can push individuals to their limits, making it increasingly difficult to maintain composure and emotional control. As stress continues to mount, the risk of anger outbursts and strained relationships with colleagues become more prevalent. Moreover, prolonged exposure to workplace stressors can have a detrimental effect on overall well-being, perpetuating a cycle of frustration and negativity.

Amid workplace stressors, the struggle to control anger can have significant consequences for individuals and their professional surroundings. Suppressing emotions and bottling frustration often leads to a breaking point where even the slightest triggers can ignite explosive reactions. Unchecked anger can result in damaged relationships, compromised teamwork, missed opportunities, and hindered career growth.

Furthermore, the internal turmoil caused by suppressing anger affects mental and physical health, increasing stress levels and decreasing overall wellbeing. These circumstances call for reflection on the importance of fostering a work environment that acknowledges and addresses employees' emotional challenges, offering constructive channels for anger management, and promoting open dialogue to navigate workplace stressors effectively.

Given these stressors, it is crucial for individuals to prioritize their well-being in the face of workplace challenges. Actively managing stress and developing effective anger management techniques should be seen as essential tools for navigating the demands of the workplace. Seeking support, whether through stress reduction practices, maintaining a healthy work-life balance, or utilizing open communication channels, becomes vital. By taking ownership of their emotional health, individuals can foster an environment that empowers and supports their efforts to control anger. This, in turn, creates a healthier and more sustainable work-life integration.

WORKPLACE ANXIETY AND BURNOUT

Workplace anxiety and burnout have significant repercussions on individuals' overall well-being and emotional regulation, affecting both their personal and professional lives. When anxiety takes hold in the workplace, it disrupts individuals' sense of stability and control. The constant worry and fear associated with anxiety lead to heightened stress levels, sleep disturbances, and potentially physical health problems. Managing emotions becomes challenging as anxiety impairs individuals' ability to regulate their feelings effectively, resulting in heightened irritability, anger, or sadness. These emotional struggles strain relationships and hinder their ability to navigate workplace dynamics successfully.

On the other hand, burnout gradually erodes individuals' emotional control and resilience. The chronic exhaustion and disillusionment accompanying burnout make it challenging to maintain a positive outlook and cope with stress effectively. As burnout intensifies, individuals may experience emotional detachment, lose interest in their work, and develop a sense of cynicism or depersonalization toward colleagues and clients. This emotional detachment further impairs their ability to regulate emotions, leading to emotional volatility, apathy, or numbness.

The effects of workplace anxiety and burnout extend beyond the workplace, seeping into individuals' personal lives. The strain and emotional toll of these conditions impact their relationships with family and friends, as they may struggle to find the energy or emotional capacity to engage in personal connections fully. Moreover, the chronic stress and emotional dysregulation associated with workplace anxiety and burnout can contribute to the development or exacerbation of mental health conditions like depression and anxiety disorders, significantly impacting individuals' emotional well-being.

Workplace Anxiety

Workplace anxiety can significantly impact anger management, creating an environment where negative emotions and impulsive reactions can escalate. When individuals experience high anxiety levels in the workplace, their ability to regulate their feelings becomes compromised. The constant pressure, uncertainty, and overwhelming demands can push individuals to their limits, increasing the likelihood of anger outbursts and destructive behaviors. This toxic cycle of workplace anxiety and anger perpetuates a hostile work environment, strains interpersonal relationships, and hinders productivity and collaboration.

One detrimental effect of workplace anxiety on anger management is impaired rational thinking and decision-making processes. Tension heightens sensitivity to perceived threats and triggers, causing individuals to interpret neutral or ambiguous situations as hostile. This cognitive distortion fuels anger and leads to impulsive and irrational responses, further escalating conflicts and undermining effective problem-solving.

The impaired ability to think clearly and make sound judgments due to workplace anxiety intensifies anger and hampers the development of constructive solutions to workplace challenges.

Moreover, the chronic experience of workplace anxiety erodes emotional resilience and exacerbates anger related issues. When individuals continuously face high levels of stress and anxiety in their professional lives, their emotional resources become depleted, making it increasingly difficult to manage and regulate anger. The accumulated stress from ongoing workplace anxiety lowers the threshold for anger, resulting in heightened reactivity to minor frustrations or perceived slights. This heightened anger can harm personal well-being, job performance, and relationships with colleagues and supervisors.

Workplace anxiety and unresolved anger can create a negative feedback loop, further perpetuating the cycle of distress. Individuals experiencing chronic workplace anxiety may develop a heightened sensitivity to stressors, increasing the likelihood of perceiving future workplace situations as threatening. This elevated reactivity contributes to a chronic state of anger, where even minor stressors trigger intense emotional responses. The ongoing cycle of workplace anxiety and anger becomes self-inflicting, reinforcing negative emotional patterns and hindering personal growth and professional success.

To address workplace anxiety, individuals can employ various strategies to effectively manage their symptoms. It's important to note that different techniques may work better for different individuals, and it may require some trial and error to find the most effective methods for managing anxiety symptoms. Implementing these strategies can empower individuals to take control of their stress, improve their well-being, and enhance their job performance in the workplace:

- *Identify and manage triggers*: Recognizing the specific situations, tasks, or people that trigger your anxiety in the workplace is essential. By identifying these triggers, you can develop strategies to manage or avoid them, ultimately reducing your anxiety levels.

- *Practice stress reduction techniques*: Stress reduction techniques like deep breathing exercises, meditation, or mindfulness can help calm your mind and alleviate anxiety symptoms. Regular practice of these techniques can positively impact your overall well-being.

- *Seek social support*: Building a support network within your workplace is crucial. Connecting with colleagues, supervisors, or mentors who can offer guidance and understanding provides a valuable outlet for stress and anxiety. Having someone to talk to about your concerns can provide relief and support.

- *Set realistic expectations*: Avoid setting unrealistic expectations for yourself, as this can increase anxiety. Focus on setting achievable goals and recognize that making mistakes or seeking help is a normal part of the learning and growing process.

- *Practice self-care*: Taking care of your physical and mental well-being is essential for managing workplace anxiety. Prioritize self-care activities such as regular breaks, exercise, adequate sleep, and engaging in hobbies or activities that bring you joy and relaxation. Taking care of yourself allows you to cope better with workplace stressors.

Workplace Burnout

Workplace burnout, characterized by chronic physical and emotional exhaustion, can significantly impact anger management and escalate anger-related issues. When individuals experience burnout, they often feel overwhelmed, drained, and devoid of energy, making them more susceptible to anger outbursts and hostile reactions. The prolonged and excessive stress associated with burnout can lead to emotional dysregulation, making it challenging to manage anger effectively. As a result, individuals may exhibit impulsive and aggressive behavior, damaging relationships and worsening their overall well-being.

One of the detrimental effects of workplace burnout on anger management is the erosion of patience and tolerance. Burnout can deplete individuals' emotional resources, leaving them more vulnerable to frustration and irritability. Minor setbacks or inconveniences that would typically be manageable may trigger intense anger and disproportionate reactions in individuals experiencing burnout. This diminished capacity for patience can strain professional relationships, impact teamwork, and hinder effective problem-solving, ultimately compromising workplace dynamics.

Workplace burnout often breeds cynicism and detachment, fostering a pessimistic perspective that seeps into one's outlook on work, relationships with colleagues, and client interactions. The emotional disconnection further erodes job satisfaction and can undermine professional relationships. These negative emotions can fuel anger, making individuals more prone to expressing their frustrations in destructive ways. The build-up of anger and resentment over time can lead to a toxic work environment characterized by interpersonal conflicts, decreased motivation, and reduced job satisfaction.

In addition to its impact on the workplace, burnout can profoundly affect an individual's personal life, including their ability to manage anger effectively. The exhaustion and emotional depletion caused by burnout can spill over into personal relationships, leading to strained interactions and conflicts with loved ones. Individuals experiencing burnout may find it challenging to separate work-related stress from their personal lives, resulting in heightened irritability, impatience, and anger in their interactions outside of work. The toll of burnout on personal relationships can lead to feelings of isolation, damaged connections, and reduced overall life satisfaction.

To address workplace burnout, individuals must explore the underlying causes of their negative feelings and experiences. It is crucial to identify the root cause or sources of stress and dissatisfaction in the work environment. Remember, addressing workplace burnout is a personal situation, which may require combining these strategies or other personalized approaches. Be patient with yourself and take proactive steps towards creating a healthier work-life balance and nurturing your well-being. To effectively combat workplace burnout, individuals can follow these steps:

- *Reflect and Identify*: Reflect on your experiences and identify the underlying causes of your burnout. Consider aspects of your work environment, such as excessive workload, lack of control or autonomy, insufficient support, or mismatched values. Understanding the specific factors contributing to your burnout can help you develop targeted strategies.

- *Set Boundaries and Prioritize Self-Care*: Establish clear boundaries between work and personal life to promote work-life balance. This includes setting limits on working hours, taking regular breaks, and prioritizing self-care activities that replenish your physical and emotional wellbeing. Engaging in hobbies, exercise, relaxation techniques, and spending time with loved ones can help recharge your energy.

- *Seek Support*: Contact trusted colleagues, friends, or mentors who can provide support and guidance. Discuss your feelings of burnout and seek their perspective or advice. Additionally, consider seeking professional help from therapists or coaches specializing in burnout and stress management.

- *Communicate with Supervisors and Team*: If possible, have open and honest conversations with your supervisors or team members about your burnout. Discuss your workload, responsibilities, and potential adjustments that can alleviate stress. Effective communication can lead to shared solutions and support from your colleagues.

- *Develop Coping Strategies*: Explore and implement coping strategies that work best for you. This can include stress management techniques like mindfulness meditation, deep breathing exercises, or journaling. Engaging in activities that bring you joy and relaxation outside work can also reduce stress.

- *Reassess Goals and Priorities*: Take time to reassess your goals and values, both personally and professionally. Reflect on what truly matters and consider aligning your actions and decisions accordingly. This may involve reevaluating your career path, seeking new opportunities, or making changes to create a more fulfilling work-life balance.

COPING WITHIN TOXIC WORK ENVIRONMENTS

Coping with the challenges of a toxic work environment while prioritizing one's well-being requires a proactive and intentional approach. It begins with self-awareness and recognizing the hostile environment's impact on mental and emotional health. Individuals can then implement strategies to protect their well-being, such as practicing self-care, setting boundaries, and seeking support from trusted colleagues or friends outside of work. By prioritizing their well-being, individuals can better navigate toxicity challenges and maintain their resilience in the face of adversity.

Effective communication and conflict-resolution skills are crucial when navigating negative attitudes, conflicts, and criticism in the workplace. Approaching such situations with a calm and constructive mindset, actively listening to other's perspectives, and expressing oneself assertively yet respectfully can help address conflicts and reduce the impact of toxicity on one's emotional well-being. Developing these skills empowers individuals to engage in productive dialogue, find common ground, and potentially foster positive change within the toxic work environment.

Establishing clear boundaries is essential, both in terms of personal values and professional expectations. By limiting acceptable treatment and behavior, individuals can assert their rights and foster a sense of self-respect.

Communicating boundaries effectively to colleagues and superiors help establish mutual understanding and may encourage more respectful interactions. Additionally, promoting a culture of respect and collaboration within the workplace contributes to coping with toxicity by creating an environment where open communication, teamwork, and mutual support are valued. This fosters a sense of psychological safety and can help counteract the adverse effects of a toxic work environment.

Maintaining mental health and resilience despite a toxic work environment requires a holistic approach. Engaging in stress-reducing activities outside of work, such as exercise, hobbies, or mindfulness practices, can provide a much-needed outlet for releasing tension and improving overall well-being. It is also crucial to nurture positive relationships outside of work to counterbalance the negative experiences at the workplace. Seeking professional support, such as therapy or counseling, can provide valuable guidance and coping strategies to navigate the emotional challenges associated with toxicity. Additionally, exploring alternative job opportunities or considering a career change can empower individuals to regain control over their professional lives and find a work environment that aligns with their values and promotes their well-being.

By combining self-awareness, effective communication, boundary-setting, and holistic well-being practices, individuals can cope more effectively within toxic work environments. While these strategies may not eliminate the toxicity, they empower individuals to navigate the challenges with greater resilience, protect their wellbeing, and seek opportunities for personal growth and positive change. Remember, your well-being matters, and you have the power to shape your path toward a more positive and supportive work experience. Let us explore several effective coping strategies that can help individuals deal with a negative workplace environment:

- *Practice self-care*: Engage in activities that promote mental, emotional, and physical well-being. Take care of yourself by exercising, practicing mindfulness or meditation, getting enough sleep, and taking breaks when needed.

- *Set clear boundaries*: Establish boundaries to protect your mental and emotional health. Communicate your limits and expectations to colleagues, and assertively address any violations of those boundaries. Saying no to tasks you cannot handle is essential for preserving your well-being.

- *Seek support*: Contact trusted colleagues, friends, or mentors who can provide a listening ear, advice, and emotional support. Connecting with others who understand your experiences can help you feel validated and less isolated in a hostile work environment.

- *Improve communication and conflict-resolution skills*: Develop effective communication and conflict resolution skills to navigate negative attitudes, conflicts, and criticism. Practice active listening and assertiveness while seeking win-win solutions to promote more constructive interactions.

- *Consider alternative options*: Assess the feasibility of exploring alternative job opportunities or a career change. Sometimes, removing yourself from a toxic work environment is the best longterm solution for your well-being. Develop a plan for change, such as finding a new job, speaking to HR or a supervisor about the issues, or seeking legal advice if necessary.

DIVERSITY BEYOND THE JOB

In today's fast-paced world, many individuals view their jobs as a necessary means to sustain their existence. However, it is worth questioning whether there is more to work than just a paycheck. What if we dared to challenge this perspective and delve deeper into the purpose behind our work?

Amid long work hours and societal pressures, it is easy to lose sight of personal growth and passions. We often find ourselves trapped in a cycle where work dominates our schedules, leaving little time or energy for self-discovery and pursuing what truly ignites our souls. But what if we were to reimagine our relationship with work? What if we reclaimed our identities from the clutches of job titles and career paths?

Imagine a world where we define ourselves not solely by what we do for a living but by the essence of who we are as human beings. We must recognize that our worth extends far beyond our job descriptions. Whether we are nurses, engineers, janitors, or any other profession, we all have the power to make a profound impact on the lives of others. Our work becomes a vessel for our unique talents and contributions, transcending mere transactions for survival.

Discovering our true purpose means going beyond the confines of our jobs. It involves delving deep into our core, unearthing the passions, talents, and values that resonate with our very being. It is about finding fulfillment not only in our professional endeavors but also in the meaningful acts of service we provide to humanity. By nurturing our strengths outside the workplace and cultivating a harmonious balance between our personal and professional lives, we unlock the door to a more purposeful and well-rounded existence.

MANAGING EMOTIONS IN PUBLIC

Effectively managing emotions in public requires a delicate balance between authenticity and consideration for others. It involves cultivating self-awareness to recognize and regulate our emotional reactions while empathizing with those around us and respecting social norms. By understanding the impact of our emotions on ourselves and others, we can navigate public spaces with emotional composure and contribute to a more harmonious social environment.

A crucial aspect of managing emotions in public is developing self-awareness. By being in tune with our emotions, we can recognize the signs of emotional escalation and intervene before they overpower us. This involves understanding our emotional triggers and patterns, allowing us to anticipate how certain situations may affect us and take proactive steps to regulate our emotions effectively. Techniques such as deep breathing, mindfulness, or reframing our thoughts can help maintain emotional balance.

Empathy plays a vital role in managing emotions in public. Recognizing that public spaces are shared by individuals with their own emotions and experiences allows us to consider the feelings of others. By being aware of how our emotions may impact those around us, we can regulate our behavior in a considerate and compassionate manner. This may involve finding appropriate outlets for our emotions, such as stepping away to a private space to express intense feelings or engaging in constructive dialogue to address conflicts.

Being empathetic helps create a more understanding and supportive social atmosphere. Respecting societal norms and expectations is essential when managing emotions in public. While it is important to be authentic, there are boundaries and social codes that maintain order and respect within shared spaces. Striking a balance between expressing ourselves genuinely and adhering to these conventions is crucial. This requires adapting our communication style to the context, using appropriate language, and being mindful of cultural nuances. By aligning our emotional expression with societal norms, we facilitate better communication, promote understanding, and create a more harmonious social environment.

Effectively managing emotions in public is likened to a skilled tightrope walker. It involves maintaining emotional equilibrium amidst external stimuli and triggers, just as a tightrope walker maintains balance amidst gusts of wind and distractions. This requires focus, control, and heightened awareness of our emotions and their impact. By practicing resilience and self-regulation, we can gracefully manage emotions, captivating those around us with emotional stability and poise. By cultivating self-awareness, empathy, and respect for societal norms, we navigate public spaces with emotional composure, contributing to a positive and harmonious social atmosphere.

MITIGATING PUBLIC SITUATIONS

Mitigating public situations from escalating is of utmost importance to maintain harmony, safety, and positive social interactions. When conflicts or tensions are left unchecked, they have the potential to spiral out of control, leading to harmful consequences for the individuals involved and the broader community. By actively working to de-escalate these situations, we create an environment conducive to understanding, empathy, and resolution.

One key reason for mitigating public situations from escalating is to ensure the well-being and safety of all parties involved. When tensions rise, and conflicts intensify, the risk of physical harm or verbal abuse increases significantly. By taking proactive steps to deescalate, we minimize the potential for violence or injury. This not only protects the individuals directly involved but also preserves the overall safety and peace of the public space.

Furthermore, de-escalating public situations promotes a culture of respect, understanding, and cooperation. When conflicts are allowed to escalate, it often results in a breakdown of communication, a deepening of divisions, and a fostering of hostility. By stepping in and working to de-escalate, we foster an atmosphere where open dialogue, empathy, and compromise can prevail. This not only resolves the immediate conflict but also sets a positive example for others, encouraging peaceful resolutions and constructive engagement in future interactions.

Mitigating public situations from escalating also helps to preserve relationships and prevent long-lasting damage. In public spaces, conflicts can involve individuals with ongoing interactions, such as coworkers, neighbors, or community members. Allowing these conflicts to escalate without intervention can strain relationships and create a toxic environment. By stepping in and de-escalating, we can repair and rebuild these relationships, promoting forgiveness, understanding, and healing.

This not only benefits the individuals involved but also strengthens the fabric of the community as a whole.

Additionally, by de-escalating public situations, we contribute to a more positive and inclusive society. Individuals from diverse backgrounds, cultures, and perspectives share public spaces. Conflicts that escalate can perpetuate stereotypes, discrimination, and a climate of fear and hostility. By actively working to deescalate, we promote an atmosphere of acceptance, empathy, and respect for all. This helps to build bridges between individuals, bridge gaps in understanding, and foster a sense of unity and belonging.

In certain circumstances, it may be necessary to remove yourself entirely from a situation for your safety. If someone's behavior becomes threatening or dangerous, prioritize your well-being and seek assistance from security personnel or law enforcement. It is crucial to stay composed and regulate your emotions to deescalate public conflicts and create an atmosphere of peace and harmony. Kindness and compassion can also play a significant role in diffusing tense situations, as they promote understanding and empathy among those involved.

In our current society, public interactions can sometimes feel like navigating a complex maze. People from different backgrounds, cultures, and perspectives converge in public spaces, bringing a range of opinions and emotions. Tensions can arise, conflicts can escalate, and maintaining harmonious interactions may seem challenging. However, proven strategies have been effective in defusing conflicts, promoting understanding, and fostering cooperative relationships in such situations. By employing these strategies with care and adaptability, individuals can pave the way for meaningful connections, constructive dialogue, and a more inclusive and empathetic public sphere.

- *Active Listening*: Engage in active listening by giving your full attention to the person or people involved in the conflict. Hear their concerns, perspectives, and emotions without interrupting or judging. Reflect on what they say to ensure understanding. Active listening demonstrates respect and can help defuse tension by showing that you genuinely care about their viewpoint.

- *Empathy and Understanding*: Practice kindness by putting yourself in the other person's shoes. Try to understand their underlying motivations, fears, or frustrations. Show compassion and acknowledge their feelings, even if you may not agree with their behavior or stance. When people feel heard and understood, it can help reduce hostility and open the door to constructive dialogue.

- *Calming Techniques*: In tense situations, it is crucial to remain calm and composed. Take deep breaths, regulate your emotions, and avoid reacting impulsively. Use calming techniques such as counting to ten or visualizing a peaceful scene to help manage your emotions. Your calm demeanor can influence the atmosphere and encourage others to follow suit.

- *Nonviolent Communication*: Utilize nonviolent communication techniques to express your thoughts and concerns without escalating the conflict. Focus on expressing your feelings and needs rather than attacking or blaming others. Practice active problem-solving and seek common ground or win-win solutions. Nonviolent communication fosters respectful and constructive dialogue, reducing the chances of hostility escalating.

- *Mediation and Conflict Resolution*: If the conflict persists or becomes more complex, consider involving a trained mediator or conflict resolution professional. Mediators are impartial third parties who facilitate communication and guide individuals toward mutually acceptable solutions. They can help navigate complex issues, ensure equal participation, and promote a cooperative approach to conflict resolution.

FROM PUBLIC STRESS TO PRIVATE SERENITY

Sometimes, coping with stress in public can feel like walking on a tightrope while being scrutinized by a crowd of onlookers. The weight of their expectations and judgments can make it challenging to find the space and freedom we need to process our thoughts and emotions. That's why finding private relief is incredibly valuable. Imagine being in a bustling room with people talking, laughing, and overwhelming noise. It's nearly impossible to hear your thoughts or find a moment of peace. However, stepping away into a private room or a quiet space allows everything to become clear. Suddenly, you can breathe easier, hear your thoughts, and create room to process your emotions.

Similarly, finding private relief provides the space necessary to cope with stress and anxiety. We can disconnect from our devices, close the door, and take a deep breath. At that moment, we create our world, where we can focus on our needs and emotions without the pressure of external opinions. When feeling overwhelmed and stressed, seeking private relief is not something to be feared. Whether finding solace in a secluded natural setting or creating a tranquil space within our homes, taking that moment to breathe can bring astonishing clarity and peace. It allows us to escape the precariousness of constantly performing for others.

So, let us embrace the value of private moments, where we can recharge, find clarity, and restore our inner balance amidst the demands of the public sphere. By prioritizing our well-being and nurturing our personal sanctuaries, we can navigate the tightrope of life with grace and resilience.

CONCLUSION

In a world where emotions run deep, and interactions can be complex, the way we manage our feelings in public holds tremendous significance. It is not just a personal endeavor but a responsibility we owe to ourselves and others. Our ability to navigate this emotional terrain with empathy and self-awareness can shape the fabric of society.

Imagine a world where individuals take ownership of their emotions, embracing self-reflection and fostering understanding. A world where conflicts are resolved through compassion and differences are celebrated as a testament to our collective richness. This vision starts with each of us recognizing our power to choose our responses and influence the emotional dynamics around us.

As we embark on this journey of emotional self-mastery, we become catalysts for change. By modeling emotional intelligence and practicing empathy, we inspire others to do the same. We create ripples of understanding that extend beyond our immediate interactions, sparking a transformation that reaches far and wide.

Moreover, as we navigate the complexities of public life, we begin to appreciate the interconnectedness of our experiences. Our emotions are not isolated; they intertwine with the emotions of those around us. The way we manage our feelings has the potential to shape the emotional landscapes of others. By fostering emotional well-being within ourselves, we create a space for others to do the same.

In this world, public spaces become sanctuaries of emotional exploration and growth. They become platforms for authentic connection, where vulnerability is met with compassion and understanding. The tapestry of humanity is woven with threads of empathy, acceptance, and resilience, creating a more harmonious and compassionate society.

So, let us begin this transformative journey, where we embrace the power of emotional management in public. Together, we can rewrite the narrative, creating a world where emotions are not feared but embraced, where conflicts are resolved with empathy, and where the symphony of human emotions weaves a melody of unity and understanding.

CHAPTER 6

FORGIVING AND LETTING GO

I t is not uncommon to experience overwhelming anger and frustration, accompanied by deep pain and hurt. When we feel wronged, it can be a tremendous challenge to let go of lingering resentment. However, I invite you to consider the potential of forgiveness to bring healing and liberation into your life. Forgiveness can mend the wounds within us and set us free from the burdens that weigh us down.

In moments of anger and frustration, it is important to acknowledge that these emotions are natural responses to the pain we have endured. We may have been treated unjustly or betrayed, leaving us with a lingering sense of hurt. The journey of forgiveness begins by recognizing that these emotions, while valid, do not have to define our lives indefinitely.

Forgiveness is a deeply personal journey influenced by our unique experiences and circumstances. It is essential to recognize that not every situation or experience can be easily forgiven, and it is ultimately up to each individual to determine when the time is right for forgiveness. While it may be challenging, forgiveness has the power to bring healing and solace to our hearts, enabling us to release the negative emotions that weigh us down.

Letting go of pain, hurt, resentment, and anger is a complex and ongoing process that individuals must grapple with daily to maintain emotional stability. There is no one-size-fits-all approach or definitive guidebook for navigating these deeply intertwined emotions. In order to successfully let go of these burdens, its crucial to let everything naturally process. Allow yourself the time and space to acknowledge your emotions without judgement. Embrace the ups and downs, knowing that this process is beneficial for your emotional well-being.

THE ART OF LETTING GO

Letting go is an art because it requires skillful mastery and intentional practice. It involves delicately navigating the complexities of our emotions and attachments, consciously releasing what no longer serves us. Just like an artist skillfully creates a masterpiece, letting go requires us to tap into our inner wisdom, cultivate self awareness, and make conscious choices to detach from anger, resentment, and negative emotions. It is a transformative process that requires patience, resilience, and a deep understanding of ourselves. Through the art of letting go, we liberate ourselves, create space for healing and growth, and open ourselves to the beauty and possibilities that lie beyond our attachments.

The art of letting go invites us to cultivate self awareness and develop a deeper understanding of our thoughts, emotions, and patterns of attachment. It involves recognizing that holding onto anger, resentment, or pain only perpetuates suffering and inhibits personal growth. By consciously letting go, we free ourselves from negative emotions, liberating our energy and opening space for healing, development, and new possibilities.

Letting go is not synonymous with forgetting or dismissing the past. It is about acknowledging the pain or disappointment, learning from the experiences, and choosing not to be defined or consumed by them. It allows us to release the grip of control, allowing life to unfold naturally and embrace the unknown of all things.

Picture yourself about to embark on a flight to your dream travel destination. Imagine standing at the check-in counter, struggling to lift your bulging suitcase onto the scale. It's filled with unnecessary items you've accumulated over time—past grievances, regrets, and unresolved conflicts. As you attempt to lift it, you realize how the weight prevents you from moving forward effortlessly.

Then you realize unloading excess weight from your luggage is like letting go of negative emotions before checking it in at the airport. Just as the weight of the luggage becomes burdensome and hinders your journey, the emotional baggage you carry throughout life can weigh you down and impede your personal growth and happiness.

Similarly, carrying emotional baggage from the past—grudges, pain, and negative experiences—makes it challenging to navigate through life's journey smoothly. It drains your energy, affects your relationships, and limits your ability to embrace new opportunities. Just as an overweight suitcase incurs extra fees and delays, emotional baggage incurs emotional costs and holds you back from living a fulfilling life.

When you let go of unnecessary emotional baggage, it's like unpacking heavy items from your suitcase and leaving them behind. You free yourself from the burden, allowing you to move forward with greater ease and joy. By releasing that weight, you create space for new experiences, positive emotions, and healthier relationships.

Letting Go of Anger and Resentment

When you find yourself consumed by anger and resentment, ask yourself: Is it beneficial to hold onto these negative emotions as if they were a lifeline, gripping them with all your might? Are you genuinely justified in your anger, firmly convinced that you have been wronged and that the other person deserves your wrath? Consider the consequences of holding onto anger and resentment – how does it impact yourself and the people around you? Are there healthier alternatives than clinging to these negative emotions? Can you envision a different path where you release the weight of anger and resentment? Reflect on these questions as you navigate the complexities of anger and resentment. Embracing the art of letting go opens you to the transformative power of forgiveness and emotional liberation.

When anger and resentment consume you, it may feel natural to hold onto those negative emotions tightly, believing they are justified and deserved. However, clinging to anger and resentment only harms yourself and those around you. The path to healing lies in the art of letting go. By releasing the grip of negativity, you free yourself from the burden of resentment and open up space for growth and healing. Letting go does not mean forgetting or condoning the hurt, but rather, it's a powerful act of self-care and liberation. You can release the weight of anger and resentment and embrace the transformative power of forgiveness and inner peace.

Letting go of anger and resentment offers many benefits that positively impact our well-being and relationships. Releasing anger allows us to free ourselves from the emotional burden that weighs us down. When we hold onto anger, it can consume our thoughts and energy, leading to increased stress, tension, and even physical health issues. Letting go of anger liberates us from this heavy load, enabling us to experience a greater sense of inner peace and emotional freedom.

Letting go of resentment allows us to break free from negativity and bitterness. When we hold onto resentment, we continuously revisit past grievances, keeping wounds open and hindering our ability to move forward. By releasing resentment, we create space for healing and personal growth. We can redirect our energy towards more positive endeavors and focus on building healthier relationships and a brighter future.

Another significant benefit of letting go of anger and resentment is the improvement it brings to our relationships. When we carry unresolved anger and resentment towards others, it poisons our interactions and prevents genuine connection. By letting go of these negative emotions, we open the door to forgiveness, empathy, and compassion. This paves the way for healthier and more fulfilling relationships characterized by understanding, trust, and cooperation.

Letting go of anger and resentment also fosters personal growth and self-empowerment. It allows us to take control of our emotional state and break free from the role of a victim. By releasing these negative emotions, we reclaim our power and sense of agency over our lives. This newfound empowerment opens doors to personal development, self-discovery, and pursuing our goals and aspirations.

Additionally, letting go of negative emotions empowers us to live a more authentic and joyful life. By releasing anger and resentment, we let go of the negative filters that cloud our perception of reality. When we release anger and resentment, we create space for tranquility and harmony within ourselves. Instead of being consumed by negative emotions, we find solace in acceptance, forgiveness, and self-compassion. We become more attuned to gratitude, positivity, and the beauty that surrounds us. This shift in perspective allows us to savor life's precious moments, appreciate the present, and navigate life's challenges with a sense of calm and balance.

The process of letting go requires courage, self-compassion, and a willingness to embrace change. Remember, this is a personal and empowering journey, and by taking these steps, you open the door to a life of greater peace, authenticity, and emotional well-being. Be gentle with yourself as you begin to make changes and celebrate each small step forward. If you find yourself ready to release the weight of anger, resentment, and emotional baggage, here are some essential steps to help you begin this transformative process.

- *Self-reflection and awareness*: Start by acknowledging and identifying the emotions, thoughts, and beliefs that you want to let go of. Take time to understand the root causes and triggers behind them.

- *Acceptance and forgiveness*: Practice accepting what has happened and forgiving yourself and the others involved. Understand that holding onto anger and resentment only hinders your growth and well-being.

- *Mindfulness and present moment awareness*: Cultivate mindfulness practices such as meditation or deep breathing exercises to bring yourself into the present moment. Focus on what you can control now rather than dwelling on the past or worrying about the future.

- *Release attachments and expectations*: Let go of attachments to specific outcomes, people, or situations. Recognize that clinging to expectations can lead to disappointment and frustration. Embrace the idea that life is ever-changing and that you have the power to adapt and let go.

- *Self-care and self-compassion*: Prioritize self-care activities that nurture your physical, mental, and emotional well-being. Practice self-compassion by treating yourself with kindness, understanding, and forgiveness.
- *Seek support*: Contact trusted friends, family, or professionals who can provide guidance, encouragement, and a listening ear. Support groups or therapy can be valuable resources to help you navigate the challenges of letting go.

Letting Go of Grudges

Are you carrying the weight of a grudge, allowing it to become a part of your identity? It's understandable to feel justified in your anger and resentment but holding onto a grudge only hurts you in the long run. Letting go of a grudge doesn't mean you forget what happened or excuse the other person's actions. Instead, it's a conscious choice to release yourself from the negative emotions accompanying it. By letting go, you liberate yourself from anger and resentment, allowing room for healing and growth. Rather than dwelling on the past, you can redirect your energy towards constructive practices and focus on the present. Letting go of a grudge is a powerful act of self-care and self-preservation, enabling you to move forward with lighter steps, unencumbered by the weight of past grievances.

Holding a grudge is like drinking poison and eagerly awaiting the other person's suffering. The more you cling to it, the more it corrodes you from within, infecting your mind and heart with bitterness and anguish. While the grudge may have seemed justified initially, it gradually poisons your very being, leaving you hollow and isolated. Like a potent toxin, a grudge seeps into all aspects of your life, tainting your relationships, work, and overall well-being. It's time to break free from the toxic grip of a grudge and relinquish the pain and resentment that have hindered your progress. By embracing forgiveness and releasing the grievance, you administer an antidote to the poison, liberating yourself from its grasp and granting yourself the opportunity to heal and forge ahead.

The first step in letting go of a grudge is acknowledging and validating one's emotions. It is essential to recognize the feelings of anger, hurt, and resentment that have been harbored. By accepting these emotions, individuals can create a space for self-reflection and better understand their experiences and triggers.

Once emotions have been acknowledged, it is essential to shift the focus from dwelling on the past to embracing the present moment. This involves consciously choosing to let go of rumination and repetitive thoughts that fuel the grudge. Engaging in mindfulness practices, such as meditation or deep breathing exercises, can help individuals redirect their attention to the present and cultivate inner peace.

A critical aspect of letting go of a grudge is developing empathy and compassion towards oneself and the person or situation that caused the hurt. This does not mean condoning the actions that led to the grievance but rather understanding that everyone is fallible and capable of making mistakes. By practicing self-compassion and extending empathy to the other party, individuals can release the burden of anger and resentment and open themselves up to healing.

Forgiveness is a powerful tool in the process of letting go. It is important to note that forgiveness does not imply forgetting or excusing the actions that caused the grudge. Instead, it is a conscious choice to release the negative emotions associated with the grievance and move toward emotional healing. Forgiveness is a personal journey and may take time, but it liberates individuals from the chains of resentment and allows them to reclaim their emotional well-being.

Sometimes, seeking closure through communication can help let go of a grudge. Engaging in an open and honest conversation with the person involved can provide an opportunity for both parties to express their feelings and perspectives. This dialogue allows for understanding, empathy, and the potential for reconciliation. However, it is important to approach such conversations with a willingness to listen and focus on finding a resolution rather than perpetuating conflict.

Finally, seeking support from trusted individuals, such as friends, family, or therapists, can be instrumental in the process of letting go. They can offer guidance, perspective, and a safe space for individuals to express their emotions. Supportive individuals can provide encouragement, help reframe negative thoughts, and offer valuable insights that contribute to releasing the grudge.

Letting Go of Trauma

Letting go of trauma is a deeply personal journey that cannot be imposed or dictated by others. It is a decision you must make for yourself when you reach a place of emotional readiness. Just as the impact of trauma is unique to each individual, so is the process of healing and letting go. It requires an unwavering commitment to your well-being and an acknowledgment that you deserve to be free from the weight of the past.

Letting go of trauma is not a sign of weakness or denial but a courageous act of reclaiming your power and finding a path to healing. It takes immense strength to confront the painful memories, emotions and triggers that trauma brings forth. It is a testament to your resilience and innate capacity to transcend the darkness that has overshadowed your life.

No one else can truly understand the depth of your pain or the intricacies of your healing journey. You alone hold the key to your liberation. It is a personal choice that requires self-compassion, patience, and resilience. It may involve seeking professional support, building a support network of trusted individuals, and exploring therapeutic modalities that resonate with you.

As you begin this path, remember that healing is not linear. There may be setbacks, moments of doubt, and times when the wounds resurface. But with each step forward, no matter how small, you are reclaiming fragments of your identity that trauma sought to shatter. You are rewriting the narrative, embracing your resilience, and forging a future not defined by your past.

Letting go of trauma is a process that unfolds in its own time and at its own pace. It is a journey of self-discovery, self-compassion, and self-empowerment. By choosing to let go, you are not erasing the experiences or their impact; instead, you are choosing to transcend them, rewrite your story, and reclaim your inherent right to live a life defined by healing, growth, and the limitless possibilities that lie ahead.

The first crucial step in healing from past traumas is to courageously confront and acknowledge what happened, even if it means facing difficult emotions that have been avoided or denied. It is essential to give yourself permission to experience the anger, sadness, and fear that may arise and to seek the help and support you need. By honestly confronting the reality of your past, you gain valuable insights into your resilience and capacity to overcome adversity. This process may require delving deep into your inner self, fully accepting and embracing everything you have been through, both the positive and negative.

Seeking support from others is another vital aspect of letting go of past traumas. This can involve opening up to a therapist, joining a support group, or confiding in trusted friends and family members who are nonjudgmental and capable of providing guidance. It's important to remember that everyone's healing journey is unique and finding someone to help you process your emotions and work through the pain can be immensely beneficial.

Practicing self-compassion is a crucial step in the healing process. Often, holding onto anger and resentment towards past traumas stems from self-blame, feeling inadequate, or lacking self-love. Embracing self-compassion means treating yourself with kindness and understanding, letting go of self-blame, and focusing on your personal healing and growth.

It's important to acknowledge that letting go of past trauma is a gradual process that requires courage and ongoing commitment. Healing takes time, and setbacks may occur along the way, but it's crucial to remember that you are in control of your healing journey. You have the power to release the pain and anger associated with past traumas. You deserve to live a life unburdened by the weight of those experiences. Always remind yourself of your inner strength and your ability to overcome any obstacle that comes your way.

REDEFINING THE IMPACT OF TRAUMA

Growing up in a traumatic environment can profoundly shape an individual's life, but it does not predetermine their future. This is exemplified in the story of two brothers who experienced traumatic events in a broken household and encountered similar challenges as they transitioned into adulthood. Despite their shared upbringing, the brothers embarked on divergent paths, highlighting the powerful influence of personal choices and resilience.

The elder brother chose to confront his past directly and acknowledged the pain he had endured, which helped him seek support to help him. He channeled his creativity and compassion, using his past as fuel to impact the world positively. Recognizing that his upbringing did not define him, he committed himself to personal growth. He transformed his pain into resilience, pouring his heart and soul into his work and finding solace in helping others. His traumatic experiences became a source of strength, propelling him toward success and fulfillment. Through his determination and unwavering spirit, he overcame obstacles and found his true calling.

Conversely, the younger brother allowed his traumatic experiences to become an excuse for his failures and self-destructive behavior. Rather than seeking help and addressing his pain, he chose to suppress it, leading to a cycle of despair. His past became a defining characteristic, holding him back from personal growth and perpetuating a pattern of self-destruction. The obstacles in his adulthood only reinforced his negative beliefs as he remained shackled by his past. While it is disheartening to witness such a trajectory, it emphasizes the crucial role of support, healing, and self-awareness in overcoming the impact of trauma.

The tale of these two brothers highlights the power of choice and resilience in shaping one's destiny. Despite facing identical trauma, their responses and outcomes diverged significantly. When asked what fueled his success, the first brother would reply, "It's because I came from a broken home." Conversely, when asked why he chose a life of self-destruction, the second brother would respond, "It's because I came from a broken home." These two responses, stemming from the same background, resulted in entirely different outcomes. Their interpretations of this experience were significantly different. The first brother embraced his complicated past as a source of inspiration and strength, which propelled him toward success. In contrast, the second brother allowed the same circumstances to become a crutch, perpetuating a cycle of self-destruction.

This story compels us to recognize that while our experiences undeniably shape us, we have the power to choose our response to them. We can either allow adversity to break us down or transform it into a source of fortitude and motivation, positively impacting the world. The contrasting outcomes of these two brothers underscore the profound significance of personal agency and the transformative potential that lies within us. Though the past exerts its influence, we possess the capacity to transcend its limitations and forge our path toward resilience, growth, and making a meaningful difference in the world.

UNDERSTANDING FORGIVENESS

Forgiveness is a powerful and transformative force that arises from the intricate fabric of our human experience. It entails consciously letting go of anger, resentment, and bitterness toward those who have caused us pain. It is important to note that forgiveness does not mean forgetting or downplaying the hurt. Instead, it is a deliberate choice to free ourselves from the burden of negative emotions that hold us captive.

By replacing vengeance with compassion, understanding, and empathy, we begin to heal and gain inner peace and liberation.

It is important to differentiate between forgiveness and reconciliation, as these terms are often used interchangeably but encompass distinct processes. Forgiveness is a personal decision, whereas reconciliation involves rebuilding the relationship with the person who harmed us. Reconciliation requires mutual effort and agreement, while forgiveness is a path that we undertake individually. While forgiveness can create a pathway toward reconciliation, it does not guarantee it. Understanding this distinction is essential in navigating the complexities of forgiveness and avoiding confusion between forgiveness and the restoration of relationships.

Forgiveness embodies strength and resilience, an affirmation of our power. It is not a sign of weakness but a courageous act of self-love. By forgiving, we break free from the chains of anger and resentment, embracing the freedom to live fully in the present moment. This process is unique to each individual, unfolding at its own pace. It requires patience, self-compassion, and a willingness to confront our vulnerabilities. By honoring forgiveness as a sacred act of self-care, we open ourselves to profound healing and the potential for restoring broken connections.

Forgiveness is not about erasing the past but about rewriting the future. It empowers us to transform wounds into opportunities for personal growth and transformation. By embracing forgiveness, we create pathways to deep healing, genuine connection, and a life imbued with compassion and purpose. With courage, we embrace forgiveness, liberating ourselves from the weight of the past and unearthing the boundless potential within. As we embark on this transformative journey, we not only heal ourselves but also ignite a ripple effect of forgiveness and love, touching the lives of others and contributing to a more compassionate and harmonious world.

PRACTICING FORGIVENESS

Practicing forgiveness requires deep introspection and a willingness to confront our own emotions. It starts with acknowledging the pain and hurt caused by others and allowing ourselves to feel the full range of emotions that arise. It entails recognizing that holding onto anger and resentment only perpetuates our suffering. It's also about taking responsibility for our actions, making amends where necessary, and then letting go of the past. True forgiveness involves a conscious decision to release negative emotions and let go of the desire for revenge or retribution.

Practicing forgiveness also requires setting healthy boundaries and practicing assertiveness. It does not mean tolerating or enabling harmful behavior. Forgiveness is not about becoming a doormat or allowing others to take advantage of us. It involves communicating our feelings assertively and respectfully expressing our needs. It may also include establishing boundaries to protect ourselves from future harm.

The act of forgiveness is not a one-time event but an ongoing commitment to emotional well-being. It is not uncommon for the guilt and pain associated with the past to resurface after you have forgiven someone or yourself. This highlights the ongoing nature of forgiveness and the need to address and heal emotional wounds continually. It involves self-reflection, seeking support from loved ones or professionals, and utilizing therapy or mindfulness practices. It is important to remember that forgiveness does not have a set timeline and varies for each individual and situation. In forgiveness, we embark on a transformative journey that allows us to find inner peace and embrace a future filled with compassion and growth.

When practicing forgiveness, it is important to recognize its complexity and the various elements involved, such as self-reflection, empathy, and open communication. To help navigate this journey and gain a deeper understanding of forgiveness toward oneself and others, consider asking the following questions:

- What were the specific actions or events causing the hurt or pain, and how did they impact me, or the other person involved? Understanding the nature and extent of the harm is crucial for acknowledging its impact.

- What were the circumstances surrounding the situation, and what emotions did I or the other person experience? Exploring the emotional landscape helps to develop empathy and compassion for oneself and others.

- What were the motivations or intentions behind the hurtful behavior, and are they understandable or justifiable? Examining the reasons behind the actions can offer insight into the complexities of human behavior and foster understanding.

- In what ways did I or the other person contribute to the situation, and how could it have been handled differently to prevent or address the hurt? Recognizing personal accountability and considering alternative approaches encourages growth and learning from the experience.

- What negative emotions or beliefs have I been holding onto due to the hurt, and how are they impacting my relationships or mental wellbeing? Identifying and addressing lingering negative feelings or thoughts is essential for personal healing and creating healthier relationships.

- What would it take to forgive myself or the other person, and what changes in actions or behaviors would be necessary? Defining the conditions for forgiveness allows for setting realistic expectations and goals.

- How can I work towards repairing or improving the relationship, and how can I effectively communicate my forgiveness? Exploring ways to rebuild trust and foster understanding can facilitate the process of reconciliation and healing.

- How can I prioritize self-care and self-compassion during the forgiveness process, and what resources or support do I need? Recognizing the importance of self-care, seeking help from loved ones or professionals, and utilizing resources such as therapy or mindfulness practices can facilitate the forgiveness journey.

Forgiving Yourself

Self-forgiveness is a challenging process that contributes significantly to personal growth and healing. It requires us to acknowledge and take responsibility for our mistakes and flaws. We must understand that, as humans, we are fallible and prone to errors. In cultivating self-compassion and kindness, we recognize our worthiness of forgiveness and love.

Self-forgiveness is an essential aspect of the forgiveness journey, but it should not be confused with forgetting or condoning past actions. Instead, self-forgiveness is about freeing ourselves from the burden of guilt and shame associated with our mistakes. It is a gift we give to ourselves, allowing us to experience greater peace, happiness, and personal growth. When we choose to forgive ourselves, it is natural to feel a range of emotions, including regret, sadness, or anger. It is important to acknowledge and allow ourselves to feel these emotions without getting stuck in them.

Rather than dwelling on past mistakes, it is beneficial to shift our focus to the present moment and take action to make amends and move forward. Confronting our mistakes and acknowledging our imperfections leads to a deeper understanding of ourselves. It enables us to develop a more positive self-image and create a path toward a brighter future.

Through self-forgiveness, we gradually let go of the grip our past has on us, embrace personal growth, and find inner peace.

Self-forgiveness is an essential practice that supports personal growth and healing. It's important to approach this process with patience and understanding. Be gentle and understanding with yourself as you navigate through these steps of self-forgiveness. Remember that it is a journey and realize that setbacks and emotions arise along the way. If you find that the process becomes overwhelming or you need additional support, don't hesitate to reach out to loved ones or mental health professionals. Here are some practical steps to help you cultivate self-forgiveness:

- *Reflection and Acknowledgment*: Taking the time to reflect on the situation and acknowledging the impact of your actions is crucial. It involves being honest about what happened and the emotions that arise.

- *Responsibility and Accountability*: Accepting responsibility for your actions and their consequences is a significant step. It shows a willingness to own up to your mistakes and take accountability for the harm caused.

- *Self-Compassion and Kindness*: Practicing self-compassion involves treating yourself with kindness, understanding, and forgiveness. It means embracing your humanity and recognizing that making mistakes is a part of growth.

- *Learning and Growth*: Seeing mistakes as opportunities for learning and personal development is essential. Embrace the lessons and insights from the experience and commit to making positive changes moving forward.

- *Release and Letting Go*: Finally, the process of self-forgiveness involves releasing self-judgment, guilt, and shame. It means freeing yourself from the weight of the past and allowing yourself to move forward with a sense of peace and renewed purpose.

Reflections of Forgiveness

Looking in the mirror may seem counterintuitive, but it can be a powerful tool for achieving self-forgiveness. When we look in the mirror, we confront ourselves with unflinching honesty, acknowledging our flaws, imperfections, and the consequences of our actions. This raw vulnerability opens the door to growth, healing, and self-forgiveness. By gazing at our reflection, we can recognize the harm we have caused ourselves and others.

While you stand before a mirror, gazing at your reflection with a heavy heart, you see a myriad of emotions reflected at you. There may be a glimmer of pain in your eyes, a testament to your struggles and the burden you may carry in your heart. As you look into the mirror, it doesn't lie or judge; it simply reflects what's there. It shows not only your flaws but also your strengths, your beauty, and your uniqueness. You see the lines on your face, etched by laughter and tears, telling stories of joy and sorrow. Imperfections and blemishes remind you of battles fought and scars healed.

In this moment of reflection, you realize that you are not defined solely by your mistakes, regrets, or shortcomings. You see yourself as a human being, flawed and imperfect yet capable of growth, change, and self-improvement. The mirror reveals the potential within you, the resilience that has carried you through hardships, and the capacity for compassion and kindness that resides in your heart.

With this newfound understanding, you gather the courage to forgive yourself for what you've done wrong, the people you may have unintentionally hurt, and the opportunities you feel you've missed. You acknowledge your humanity, embracing its complexities and contradictions. The reflection in the mirror becomes a source of solace and acceptance, reminding you that you deserve love, understanding, and forgiveness—both from others and, most importantly, from yourself.

Forgiving Others

Forgiving others is a profound and courageous act, especially for individuals with anger management issues. Anger can be overwhelming, trapping individuals in a cycle of resentment and pain. However, choosing forgiveness helps individuals to reclaim power and break free from anger. Forgiveness enables individuals to confront their vulnerabilities, confront anger triggers, and learn to respond with empathy and understanding. Embracing forgiveness empowers individuals to take control of their emotions, which enhances personal growth and development.

While dealing with anger, forgiving others can be a decisive step toward emotional liberation. Anger is often a defense mechanism, shielding us from vulnerability and pain. By forgiving, we acknowledge our wounds and let go of the negative emotions that bind us. This release of pent-up resentment frees us from the heavy burden of anger, allowing us to heal and grow. In forgiving, we reclaim our emotional well-being and refuse to be defined by past grievances.

Furthermore, forgiveness has the potential to impact our relationships positively. When we choose to forgive, it fosters an environment of understanding, compassion, and empathy within our interactions with others. Holding onto grudges with anger erects walls between us and others, perpetuating cycles of conflict and hostility. By choosing forgiveness, we dismantle these barriers and open the door to healthier interactions. By letting go of resentment and grievances, we open the door for reconciliation and the rebuilding of trust. Forgiveness promotes more beneficial communication, conflict resolution, and the ability to move forward together. It allows us to cultivate deeper connections and strengthen our bonds with those around us, ultimately creating more gratifying relationships.

While forgiveness may be a challenging and complex process, it has the potential to bring about profound changes in one's life. It allows individuals to let go of anger, hurt, and grief, restoring peace of mind and promoting emotional well-being. As the Dalai Lama wisely observed, developing negative feelings toward those who have caused us suffering destroys our inner peace. However, by choosing forgiveness, we can experience a calmness of mind and embrace a life that is both affirming and transformative.

Take time to reflect on your wounds and the impact they have had on your life. Understand that holding onto anger and resentment only prolongs your suffering. Recognize the transformative power of forgiveness in breaking free from this cycle. Acknowledge that forgiveness does not condone or forget the actions that caused pain but liberates you from the grip of bitterness.

Develop empathy by considering the complexities of human beings and the circumstances that may have influenced the actions of those who hurt you. Forgiveness is about understanding and compassion rather than excusing or justifying their behavior. This shift in perspective allows you to detach from the personalization of the offense and opens the door to forgiveness.

Prioritize your emotional well-being throughout the forgiveness journey. Engage in self-care practices that promote healing and inner peace. Take time for activities that bring you joy, relaxation, and rejuvenation.

Embrace self-love as a foundation for forgiveness. Treat yourself with kindness, understanding, and forgiveness. Release any self-blame or guilt that may be hindering your ability to forgive. Remember, forgiving others starts with forgiving yourself.

To further support your forgiveness journey, engage in reflective journaling using prompts to explore your emotions and thoughts. Write a letter expressing your feelings to the person who hurt you, even if you don't send it. Explore the impact of resentment on your wellbeing and consider the benefits of letting go.

Cultivate gratitude by writing down positive aspects of your life. Practice visualization techniques to release negative emotions and foster empathy. Imagine a peaceful setting and visualize yourself releasing the burden of resentment with each breath. Step into the shoes of the person who hurt you and see them as a flawed human being with their struggles. Cultivate empathy and understanding through these visualizations.

Additionally, embrace guided meditations focused on forgiveness and compassion. Practice loving-kindness meditation, directing forgiveness towards yourself, the person who hurt you, and others. Cultivate compassion by recognizing the shared human experience of suffering and healing. These guided meditations will support you in fostering forgiveness from within.

Throughout your journey, explore real-life stories of individuals who have found healing and hope through forgiveness. Learn from the experiences of those who forgave even in the face of immense pain. Discover the resilience and strength that forgiveness can bring, inspiring you on your forgiveness journey. Finally, acknowledge that forgiveness is not always easy, and you may encounter setbacks. Understand that healing takes time and patience. Address common challenges such as fear of being hurt again and the struggle to rebuild trust. Stay committed and resilient, knowing that forgiveness is a gradual process.

Forgiving others is a complex and personal process that requires careful consideration and introspection. While different strategies and techniques involved in forgiveness may vary from person to person, there are key elements that can help towards letting go of resentment and finding inner peace. By engaging in these fundamental aspects, individuals can begin a transformative path of forgiveness, gradually healing emotional wounds and reclaiming their emotional wellbeing:

- *Self-reflection and self-awareness*: Developing a deep understanding of your emotions, triggers, and the impact of past wounds on your well-being is crucial. This self-reflection allows you to identify patterns, heal unresolved issues, and make informed choices towards forgiveness.

- *Acceptance*: Embracing the reality that the past cannot be changed and accepting that forgiveness is a choice is vital. Acceptance helps you shift your focus from dwelling on what happened to taking proactive steps towards healing and growth.

- *Compassion and empathy*: Cultivating compassion for yourself and others involved in the situation is a powerful catalyst for forgiveness. Empathy allows you to see the humanity in others and understand the circumstances that may have contributed to their actions, fostering a sense of connection and understanding.

- *Setting boundaries*: Establishing and maintaining healthy boundaries is crucial for self-care and protection. Boundaries allow you to create a safe space for yourself and communicate your needs and limits effectively, preventing further harm and promoting a sense of empowerment.

- *Seek support*: Seeking support from trusted individuals, such as friends, family, or professionals, can greatly facilitate the forgiveness process. Sharing your experiences, gaining perspective, and receiving guidance from others who understand and support your journey can provide invaluable support and encouragement.

OBSTACLES TO FORGIVENESS

Anger can be a formidable obstacle on the path to forgiveness. When we hold onto our anger tightly, it becomes a consuming force that controls us, preventing us from moving forward. It whispers in our ears, fueling our resentment and convincing us that forgiveness is a sign of weakness. But what if we dared to question this narrative? What if we recognized that forgiveness is not about condoning the actions that hurt us but rather about liberating ourselves from the suffocating grip of anger? Releasing our anger, we reclaim our power and embark on a transformative healing journey.

Obstacles to forgiveness can present significant challenges on our path towards healing and inner peace. These obstacles are deeply personal and can vary in intensity and complexity for each individual. One of the most poignant obstacles to forgiveness is the pain we carry within us. When we have been deeply hurt or betrayed, the wounds can penetrate our very being, making it incredibly difficult to let go. The weight of this pain can anchor us to our past, reinforcing our resentment and preventing us from moving forward. It takes immense courage and vulnerability to confront these deep emotional wounds and embark on the journey of forgiveness.

Another obstacle that often looms large is the erosion of trust. When trust is lost, forgiveness may seem like an insurmountable mountain to climb. The fear of being hurt again and the skepticism that others can change or be held accountable can make us hesitant to extend forgiveness. Rebuilding trust requires patience, communication, and a willingness to navigate the complexities of vulnerability. It is a delicate process that demands self-protection and openness to the possibility of reconciliation.

A significant hurdle to forgiveness lies in our innate desire for justice. When we are mistreated, a natural inclination arises to seek fairness and retribution. We yearn for the scales to be balanced, for the other person to face the consequences of their actions. Letting go of this desire for revenge can be arduous, as it challenges our sense of fairness and justice. It requires a profound shift in perspective, realizing that forgiveness is not about condoning or excusing the behavior but freeing ourselves from the chains of resentment and allowing healing to occur.

Another obstacle that can hinder forgiveness is the difficulty of empathizing with the person who caused us harm. Understanding their perspective, acknowledging the factors that may have influenced their actions, and finding compassion within ourselves can be an arduous task. It requires us to transcend our pain and extend empathy to someone who has caused us suffering. This act of compassion can be incredibly challenging when the hurt inflicted upon us is profound or when there is a long history of pain.

Lastly, societal and cultural influences can shape our beliefs and attitudes toward forgiveness. Cultural norms, expectations from friends and family, or societal pressures to "forgive and forget" can cloud our judgment and make the forgiveness process more complex. It is crucial to recognize and challenge these external influences, allowing ourselves the space to navigate forgiveness in a way that is authentic and meaningful to our healing journey.

In navigating the obstacles to forgiveness, we must challenge ingrained beliefs, confront our deepest fears, and cultivate the courage to step into the unknown. Acknowledging these obstacles to forgiveness is essential as we strive to cultivate empathy, compassion, and healing. Through understanding and addressing these challenges with honesty and openness, we can gradually overcome them and pave the way for forgiveness to blossom within us. Though the road may be difficult, the rewards of forgiveness are profound, offering us liberation, inner peace, and the opportunity for real growth and transformation.

TECHNIQUES FOR CULTIVATING FORGIVENESS

Strategies and techniques for forgiveness can provide invaluable guidance on our journey toward healing and letting go. These practical approaches empower us to navigate the complex terrain of forgiveness and cultivate a mindset of compassion and understanding. Remember, forgiveness is a personal journey, and everyone's path is unique. Be patient with yourself, as it may take time to embrace forgiveness fully. By applying these strategies and techniques, you can cultivate a mindset of forgiveness, experience profound healing, and reclaim your inner peace.

One of the most powerful strategies is cultivating self-compassion. Studies have consistently shown that individuals who extend kindness and understanding to themselves are more likely to forgive others. By embracing self-compassion, we create a supportive and accepting environment within ourselves, acknowledging our imperfections and treating ourselves with kindness. This self-compassionate mindset lays a strong foundation for the forgiveness journey.

Practicing empathy is another essential strategy in the forgiveness process. When we genuinely try to understand the perspective and emotions of the person who hurt us, we humanize them and foster a sense of shared humanity. Research has demonstrated that empathy is pivotal in facilitating forgiveness by promoting understanding and connection. By cultivating compassion, we open ourselves to the possibility of letting go of anger and resentment.

Mindfulness and emotional awareness are powerful tools that can support forgiveness. Engaging in mindfulness practices, such as meditation and deep breathing, allows us to observe our emotions and reactions without judgment. By mindfully acknowledging our feelings of hurt and anger, we create space to respond with compassion and forgiveness. Studies have shown that individuals who practice mindfulness are more likely to experience positive changes in their ability to forgive.

Setting boundaries is a crucial strategy in the forgiveness process. While forgiveness involves letting go of resentment, it does not mean tolerating ongoing harm. By establishing clear and healthy boundaries, we protect ourselves from further hurt while creating an environment conducive to healing. Research suggests that setting boundaries is an essential component of the forgiveness journey, allowing us to prioritize our wellbeing while working towards forgiveness.

Finally, gradually releasing resentment is a proven effective strategy for forgiveness. Forgiveness is often a process that unfolds over time and taking small steps toward forgiveness can build momentum and reinforce positive changes. Starting with less significant grievances and gradually moving towards deeper wounds allows us to manage the process more effectively and sustainably. Research has shown that a gradual approach to forgiveness can yield positive outcomes and promote long-lasting healing.

CONCLUSION

As we conclude, I encourage you, the reader, to begin your forgiveness journey. Forgiveness is not a simple act, nor is it a sign of weakness. It is an act of liberation, a reclaiming of our inner peace, and a refusal to let the burdens of resentment define our lives. In choosing forgiveness, we release ourselves from the shackles of anger and bitterness, allowing our hearts to breathe again. We acknowledge that forgiveness does not condone or forget the pain caused but seeks to free ourselves from its grip, creating space for healing and growth.

Along this journey, we have encountered obstacles and challenges that have tested our resolve. We have grappled with anger, betrayal, the desire for justice, and the need to confront our shadows. Yet, within these obstacles lies the opportunity for profound transformation. By questioning societal expectations, nurturing self-compassion, practicing empathy, and setting healthy boundaries, we navigate the complexities of forgiveness with grace and resilience.

In the act of forgiving and letting go, we extend compassion not only to others but also to ourselves. We recognize that we are flawed beings, capable of causing pain just as we are capable of experiencing it. Through self-compassion, we cultivate understanding, acceptance, and forgiveness within our hearts, creating a foundation for genuine forgiveness towards others.

As we conclude this chapter, let us carry with us the profound truth that forgiveness is not a destination but an ongoing practice. It requires patience, perseverance, and a commitment to our well-being. It is a courageous choice that leads to personal growth, emotional freedom, and the restoration of relationships. In embracing forgiveness, we open ourselves to a future filled with compassion, joy, and profound connections.

May we continue to walk this path with open hearts, extending forgiveness to ourselves and others, knowing that in doing so, we contribute to the healing of our souls and the collective healing of humanity. May the wisdom gained on this journey guide us toward a life grounded in love, compassion, and humanity.

CHAPTER 7

CONTROLLING ANGER WITH COGNITIVE BEHAVIORAL THERAPY

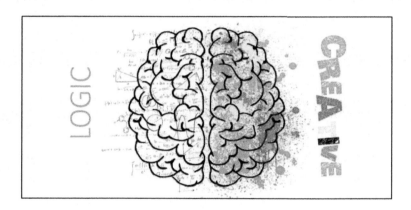

Throughout this book, we have discussed numerous techniques and strategies to manage and control anger. However, one powerful method yet to be introduced is Cognitive Behavioral Therapy (CBT). Widely regarded as one of the most effective evidence-based approaches, CBT offers long-term emotional regulation benefits that enable a positive mindset. With its focus on identifying and modifying thought patterns and behaviors, CBT empowers individuals to gain better control over their anger and experience transformations in their overall well-being. CBT offers a structured and practical approach to addressing the underlying causes of anger and developing healthier responses. By integrating CBT into our anger management journey, we open the door to lasting change and a renewed sense of inner peace.

CBT can be a lifeline for those who feel trapped by their anger, offering a way to break free from the cycle of negative thoughts, emotions, and behaviors that keep them stuck in self-destructive patterns. Through CBT, individuals can identify the root causes of their anger, understand triggers, and develop practical strategies for healthy emotional management. Moreover, CBT enables individuals to challenge negative thoughts and replace them with more realistic and positive ones, leading to a profound shift in their relationship with anger. As self-awareness grows and coping skills improve, individuals can respond to challenging situations with calmness, clarity, and confidence. The benefits of CBT extend beyond anger management, positively impacting overall mental health, reducing stress and anxiety, and enhancing relationships with loved ones.

WHAT IS COGNITIVE BEHAVIORAL THERAPY?

Cognitive Behavioral Therapy (CBT) is a therapeutic approach that focuses on the connection between our thoughts, emotions, and behaviors. It operates on the principle that our thoughts influence our feelings and actions, and by identifying and modifying negative or unhelpful thought patterns, we can achieve positive changes in our emotions and behaviors. CBT is widely regarded as one of the most effective evidence-based approaches in the field of psychology.

What makes CBT effective is its structured and practical nature. It provides individuals with specific techniques and strategies that can be applied daily. Working closely with a trained therapist, individuals learn to identify and challenge automatic negative thoughts, replacing them with more rational and positive ones. This process helps to alleviate distressing emotions and allows individuals to adopt healthier coping mechanisms.

CBT is effective because it targets the underlying causes of various psychological difficulties, including anger. It helps individuals understand the triggers that lead to anger and provides them with tools to manage and control their emotional responses. By increasing self-awareness, individuals can recognize the early warning signs of anger and intervene before it escalates into an uncontrolled outburst. Through relaxation techniques, such as deep breathing and visualization, individuals can calm themselves down and regain control over their emotions.

Numerous studies have demonstrated the efficacy of CBT in treating conditions such as anxiety disorders, depression, obsessive-compulsive disorder (OCD), post-traumatic stress disorder (PTSD), and more (Kaczkurkin & Foa, 2015). What sets CBT apart is its ability to produce long-lasting results, with many individuals experiencing significant symptom improvement in just a few sessions.

Beyond treating mental health disorders, CBT has also shown remarkable benefits in enhancing the overall quality of life. By fostering a more positive and constructive outlook, CBT can improve relationships, boost self-esteem, and enhance overall well-being. It equips individuals with the skills necessary to navigate life's challenges and stresses, making them more resilient and better equipped to handle difficult situations.

When managing anger, CBT provides a systematic and evidence-based approach. CBT emphasizes the interconnectedness of our thoughts, emotions, and behaviors, highlighting that by changing our thinking patterns, we can effectively alter our emotional responses and behaviors. Through CBT, individuals learn to identify cognitive distortions and automatic negative thoughts contributing to anger.

Individuals acquire tools and techniques to challenge and reframe these thoughts, fostering healthier perspectives and emotional regulation. Additionally, CBT underscores the significance of behavioral changes, encouraging individuals to develop and practice new coping strategies and communication skills to express their emotions constructively. By integrating these components, CBT offers a comprehensive framework for effectively managing and transforming anger.

IMPACT OF CBT WITH ANGER MANAGEMENT

CBT aims to help individuals identify and change negative thought patterns and beliefs that contribute to their anger. By gaining insight into the underlying causes of their anger, individuals can develop effective coping strategies to manage and regulate their emotions more constructively. CBT provides a structured framework that empowers individuals to take an active role in their healing process, promoting long-term positive changes in their anger management skills.

The cognitive component of CBT focuses on exploring and modifying unhelpful or distorted thought patterns related to anger. This involves identifying and challenging automatic negative thoughts, such as catastrophizing or all-or-nothing thinking, that contribute to intense anger responses. By examining the evidence for these thoughts and considering alternative perspectives, individuals can gain a more balanced and realistic view of situations, ultimately leading to more adaptive emotional responses.

The behavioral component of CBT involves addressing the behaviors associated with anger. These behaviors can vary widely from person to person and may include both verbal and physical expressions of anger. Some common examples of anger-related behaviors include yelling, screaming, physical aggression, passive-aggressive behavior, and withdrawing from social interactions.

CBT also aims to help individuals develop healthier and more constructive responses to anger triggers, allowing them to manage their anger in a way that is less harmful to themselves and others. This may include learning and practicing techniques such as relaxation exercises, assertiveness training, and problem-solving skills.

In CBT, the relationship between thoughts, emotions, and behaviors is a central focus. It recognizes that our ideas about a situation influence our emotional and behavioral responses. For example, if someone believes they must always be in control, they may become angry when they perceive a loss of control. By examining and challenging these thoughts, individuals can better understand how their thoughts contribute to anger. CBT helps individuals identify patterns of thinking that contribute to anger and teaches them to develop more adaptive and rational thoughts, leading to more appropriate emotional and behavioral responses.

By exploring the cognitive and behavioral components of CBT and understanding the relationship between thoughts, emotions, and behaviors in anger, individuals can acquire valuable skills and tools to manage their anger effectively. Through the collaborative and structured nature of CBT, individuals can make meaningful changes in their thinking patterns and behaviors, ultimately leading to improved anger management and overall well-being.

Choosing CBT for anger management issues can provide individuals with practical tools, insights, and skills to better understand and regulate their anger. CBT offers a structured and goal-oriented approach to promote positive change and enhance overall wellbeing. By addressing the underlying causes of anger and equipping individuals with practical strategies, CBT offers a pathway toward ongoing anger management and improved quality of life. Considerations for selecting CBT as a treatment approach for anger management issues encompass the following essential factors:

- *Evidence-Based*: CBT is a well-established and extensively researched therapy approach with a solid evidence base supporting its effectiveness in treating various mental health issues, including anger management problems. It encompasses scientific principles shown to produce positive and lasting results.

- *Practical Skills*: CBT equips individuals with relevant skills and strategies to manage their anger effectively. It provides concrete techniques that can be applied in real-life situations, empowering individuals to change their thoughts, emotions, and behaviors associated with anger.

- *Addressing Underlying Causes*: CBT goes beyond symptom management by addressing the underlying causes of anger. It helps individuals identify and challenge their negative thought patterns, beliefs, and interpretations that contribute to their anger. By gaining insight into these underlying factors, individuals can better understand their anger and work toward longterm change.

- *Individualized Approach*: CBT is tailored to the unique needs and circumstances of each individual. It recognizes that anger management issues can arise from various factors, such as past experiences, learned behaviors, cognitive distortions, or unhelpful coping strategies. CBT provides personalized interventions specifically designed to target the individual's specific triggers and challenges.

- *Collaborative and Empowering*: CBT adopts a collaborative and empowering approach, where the therapist and the individual work together as a team. The therapist provides guidance, support, and expertise while the individual actively participates in their treatment. This collaborative process fosters a sense of ownership and empowers individuals to take control of their anger management journey.

THE BEAUTY OF INTERNAL DIALOGUE

In the realm of cognitive behavioral therapy, the power of inner dialogue emerges as a transformative force in our lives. It is through this introspective conversation with ourselves that we unlock the potential to challenge and reshape our thoughts, ultimately influencing our emotions and behaviors. CBT encourages individuals to examine the negative or dysfunctional patterns of their inner dialogue and work towards developing more adaptive and realistic ways of thinking.

Our inner dialogue serves as a gateway to self-

awareness, illuminating the negative self-talk that often perpetuates anxiety, depression, and low self-esteem. Through the therapeutic process, clients learn to identify these destructive thoughts and actively replace them with more positive and realistic alternatives. However, rewiring our inner dialogue is not without its challenges. The automatic and ingrained nature of our thoughts can make this process daunting. Yet, with dedication and practice, clients can gain a greater sense of control over their thoughts and emotions.

Within the framework of CBT, the utilization of inner dialogue becomes empowering, allowing clients to reclaim agency in their healing journey. By becoming attuned to their negative self-talk and actively challenging it, individuals can break free from the cycle of negativity that hinders their progress. This transformative practice also cultivates a compassionate and understanding relationship with oneself, fostering kindness and empathy instead of self-judgment and criticism.

Imagine the constant stream of thoughts flowing within our minds—a mixture of blessings and curses. Yet, what if we could harness this internal dialogue and shape it into a tool for our benefit? By altering our thought patterns, we can change our emotions and actions, transforming our inner dialogue from a source of stress and anxiety into a source of empowerment.

A crucial step in this process involves questioning the validity of our thoughts. We must examine whether a thought is based on factual evidence or merely an assumption. More often than not, we realize that our negative thoughts lack a solid foundation in reality. By actively challenging these assumptions and replacing them with positive and constructive thoughts, we witness a remarkable shift in our mood and behavior.

Undoubtedly, taming the inner dialogue is no easy task. There are moments when it feels overwhelming, resembling a steady voice that won't quiet down. Yet, it's during those challenging moments that we must remind ourselves of our inherent power—the power to take control. We have the choice to listen to or dismiss that voice, consciously directing our attention towards the positive and refusing to dwell on negativity. The transformation of our inner dialogue becomes a profound journey of self-discovery and self-empowerment. By consistently challenging and reshaping our thoughts, we rewrite the script of our internal dialogue, unlocking the boundless potential for a more positive and fulfilling existence.

COGNITIVE RESTRUCTURING

In the process of cognitive restructuring, we deeply explore our thoughts and beliefs, delving into the intricate web that fuels our anger. Central to this exploration are cognitive distortions—subtle yet powerful deviations from reality that taint our perceptions and fuel our emotional responses. These distortions act as deceptive lenses through which we interpret the world, often leading us astray and intensifying our anger.

Consider a scenario where a seemingly innocuous comment from a colleague triggers an overwhelming surge of anger within us. But why does this happen? The answer lies in the distorted lenses through which we view the situation. We may engage in "all-or-nothing" thinking, perceiving the comment as a personal attack rather than a passing remark. Alternatively, we may fall into the trap of "mindreading," assuming hostile intentions behind the words without concrete evidence. These cognitive distortions skew our perception of reality, resulting in an exaggerated emotional response.

The thought-provoking aspect of cognitive restructuring lies in the challenge of identifying and questioning these cognitive distortions and unraveling their insidious influence on our anger. It calls us to scrutinize the validity of our thoughts and examine the lenses through which we perceive the world. By exploring the distortions in our thinking patterns, we begin to understand how they contribute to our anger.

We recognize that our perceptions are not always accurate reflections of reality, but somewhat biased interpretations shaped by our internal filters.

Through cognitive restructuring, we learn to question our assumptions, challenge the black-and-white thinking that narrows our perspective, and shed light on the hidden biases that color our perceptions. This process empowers us to untangle ourselves from anger driven by distorted thoughts. It encourages us to confront our cognitive biases head-on, and actively reframe our interpretations, fostering a more balanced and nuanced understanding of the world around us.

COGNITIVE DISTORTIONS

Cognitive distortions play a significant role in fueling anger, shaping our perception of events, and influencing our emotional responses. When we experience anger, our thoughts can become distorted, leading us to interpret situations in ways that may not reflect reality accurately. Three common cognitive distortions associated with anger are personalization, overgeneralization, and all-or-nothing thinking.

Personalization involves taking things personally and attributing blame to ourselves for adverse events or outcomes. It's a tendency to internalize external circumstances and hold ourselves responsible, even when other factors may be at play. Personalization can fuel anger and resentment because we may assume we are inadequate or unvalued. For example, if a colleague receives a promotion instead of us, we might automatically think it's because we lack competence, disregarding the possibility of other factors such as timing, qualifications, or organizational considerations.

Overgeneralization occurs when we draw broad conclusions based on limited experiences or a single event. It involves applying one negative instance to all similar situations, distorting our perception and amplifying anger. For example, if we disagree with a friend, we might generalize that all friendships are unreliable or untrustworthy, leading us to approach future relationships with heightened anger and suspicion. Overgeneralization overlooks the uniqueness of each situation and can perpetuate anger by painting an overly pessimistic view of the world.

All-or-nothing thinking, also known as black-and-white thinking, involves seeing things in extreme and rigid terms without acknowledging shades of gray or middle ground. It's a cognitive pattern that categorizes situations as either all good or entirely bad, leaving little room for understanding, compromise, or perspective-taking. All-or-nothing thinking can intensify anger because it promotes inflexibility and disregards the complexities of real-life situations. For example, if we make a mistake at work, we might label ourselves a complete failure, ignoring any successes or growth we have achieved.

Unraveling cognitive distortions becomes a transformative exploration of our inner landscape. This introspective journey encourages us to question and challenge the lenses through which we view the world, notably those perpetuating our anger. It is a thought-provoking endeavor that invites us to critically examine the narratives we construct and the cognitive biases that shape our perceptions. As we peel back the layers of our thoughts, we unveil the power to reshape our interpretations, fostering a greater sense of clarity and emotional well-being.

Recognizing and understanding these cognitive distortions is essential for managing anger effectively. By developing self-awareness, we can identify when these distortions are at play and challenge them to gain a more balanced and accurate perspective. Challenging these distortions involves examining the evidence supporting our thoughts, considering alternative explanations, and adopting a more flexible and realistic mindset. With practice, we can reduce the intensity of our anger, promote healthier emotional regulation, and cultivate a more harmonious inner world.

CBT TECHNIQUES TO REFRAME DISTORTED THOUGHTS

Cognitive Behavioral Therapy offers a range of techniques to help individuals reframe distorted thoughts and develop more balanced and realistic thinking patterns. These techniques are rooted in the understanding that our thoughts influence our emotions and behaviors, and by challenging and restructuring our thoughts, we can effectively manage our psychological well-being.

Reframing distorted thoughts in CBT begins with identifying and examining the cognitive distortions that contribute to negative thinking patterns. These distortions are often automatic and ingrained, causing individuals to perceive situations in ways that may not reflect reality accurately. To counter these distortions, individuals must process the evidence supporting distorted thoughts, question the validity of assumptions, and seek alternative perspectives. By doing so, individuals can develop a more balanced and objective view of themselves, others, and the world around them.

There are several reliable and commonly used CBT techniques to reframe distorted thoughts. These techniques are effective in challenging negative thinking patterns and promoting healthier cognitive processes while being applied to various situations tailored to individual needs. They provide individuals with practical tools to cultivate more accurate perspectives and promote positive emotional well-being. Let us delve into five CBT techniques that have been extensively studied and shown to be effective in helping individuals reframe distorted thoughts and manage anger more effectively.

- *Cognitive Restructuring*: Cognitive restructuring involves identifying and challenging negative or irrational thoughts and replacing them with more accurate and balanced ones. It helps individuals examine the evidence supporting and contradicting their beliefs, allowing them to develop a more realistic perspective. By questioning their assumptions and biases, individuals can reframe their thinking and reduce the impact of distorted thoughts on their emotions and behaviors.

- *Thought Record or Journaling*: Thought recording or journaling is a technique that involves keeping a record of negative thoughts, associated emotions, and the situations triggering those thoughts. It helps individuals identify recurring patterns and gain insights into their cognitive distortions. By analyzing and challenging these distorted thoughts in writing, individuals can gain clarity and develop alternative, more balanced views.

- *Thought Stopping*: Thought stopping is a technique that aims to interrupt and replace negative or unhelpful thoughts. It involves using a cue or a mental command to stop the intrusive thoughts and immediately shifting attention to a more positive or constructive focus. This technique helps individuals gain control over their thought processes and break the cycle of rumination and negative thinking.

- *Mindfulness-Based Stress Reduction (MBSR)*: MBSR combines elements of mindfulness meditation and yoga to enhance self-awareness and promote acceptance of present-moment experiences, including anger. By practicing mindfulness, individuals can observe their thoughts and emotions without judgment, allowing them to respond to anger triggers more skillfully and reduce impulsive reactions.

MBSR techniques, such as deep breathing and body scans, can help individuals develop a greater sense of calm and self-control.

- *Problem-Solving Therapy*: Problem-solving therapy focuses on identifying and implementing practical solutions to resolve anger-provoking situations. It involves a systematic approach to defining the problem, generating alternative solutions, evaluating their potential outcomes, and implementing the most appropriate one. This technique helps individuals regain control and mastery over their anger triggers, reducing frustration and promoting more constructive problem-solving strategies.

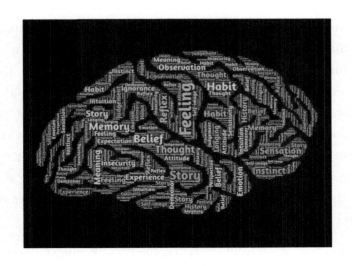

ANGER COPING SKILLS AND BEHAVIORAL TECHNIQUES

Anger often arises from underlying issues or conflicts that have gone unaddressed. By exploring problem-

solving strategies, individuals can identify and tackle the root causes of their anger, leading to more effective anger management. Problem-solving involves a systematic approach, starting with defining the problem or conflict, generating possible solutions, evaluating their potential outcomes, implementing the chosen solution, and assessing the results. This process encourages individuals to think critically and proactively about their anger triggers, considering alternative perspectives and seeking resolution. By developing strong problem-solving skills, individuals can confront challenges and conflicts constructively, fostering personal growth and conflict-resolution abilities.

Relaxation and stress reduction techniques are essential in managing anger triggers effectively. Deep breathing exercises involve taking slow, deep breaths and focusing on inhalation and exhalation, which helps activate the body's relaxation response and promotes a sense of calm.

Progressive muscle relaxation involves systematically tensing and relaxing different muscle groups to release tension and induce relaxation. Guided imagery involves visualizing calming and peaceful scenes or experiences to redirect the mind away from anger-inducing thoughts. Meditation techniques, such as mindfulness meditation, cultivate present-moment awareness and acceptance, allowing individuals to observe their anger triggers without judgment or reactivity. By regularly practicing these techniques, individuals can enhance their ability to regulate their emotional and physiological responses to anger triggers, promoting a more balanced and composed state of being.

Expressing anger assertively is crucial for effective anger management. Assertiveness training equips individuals with communication skills to express their needs, concerns, and boundaries clearly and respectfully. It involves learning to express anger directly and honestly, without aggression or passivity. Individuals learn to use declarative statements to express their emotions and needs, actively listen to other's perspectives, and seek mutually satisfactory solutions. By developing assertiveness skills, individuals can express their anger healthily and constructively, fostering open communication, understanding, and conflict resolution. This approach helps individuals avoid bottling their anger or resorting to aggressive outbursts, creating a more positive and respectful social environment.

WHY CHOOSE CBT?

CBT has shown significant positive impacts on various issues, including depression, anxiety, substance abuse, personal and professional relationships, mental health issues, and eating disorders. Extensive research supports the effectiveness of CBT, demonstrating its ability to improve the quality of life for many individuals (American Psychological Association, 2017). Compared to other forms of therapy and medication, CBT has consistently shown superior outcomes.

One of the strengths of CBT lies in its integration of scientific research and clinical practice. It combines evidence-based strategies with practical skills and techniques that individuals can apply daily. For anger management specifically, CBT equips individuals with a toolbox of practical skills such as relaxation techniques, problem-solving skills, and communication skills. By learning and practicing these skills, individuals gain a greater sense of control over their emotions and can respond to anger triggers in a more constructive and adaptive manner.

Real-life examples and empirical studies support the effectiveness of CBT in anger management. For instance, a study published in the Journal of Consulting and Clinical Psychology found that individuals who participated in a CBT-based anger management program experienced significant improvements in their ability to manage their anger compared to those who did not receive treatment (McIntyre et al., 2019). This research demonstrates that CBT can yield tangible and lasting improvements for individuals struggling with anger.

Beyond research findings, the personal experiences of individuals who have undergone CBT treatment for anger management further illustrate its effectiveness. Many individuals report that CBT has empowered them to gain better control over their emotions, leading to improved relationships and an enhanced overall quality of life. They describe feeling more confident in their ability to manage anger in real-world situations and appreciate the practical tools and strategies that CBT offers.

CBT offers a unique set of advantages that make it a compelling choice for individuals seeking effective anger management. Its practical and skills-oriented nature equips individuals with tangible tools and techniques to address their anger daily. CBT goes beyond surface-level symptom management and aims to address the underlying causes of anger. Through CBT, individuals can gain insight into the thoughts, beliefs, and behaviors contributing to their anger. By focusing on the present and providing actionable strategies, CBT empowers individuals to take an active role in their healing process.

The collaborative nature of CBT ensures a robust therapeutic alliance where the individual's unique needs and perspectives are valued and incorporated into the treatment. This personalized approach enhances the effectiveness of the therapy. Additionally, CBT's versatility allows it to be adapted to different individuals and their specific anger management needs, making it a flexible and practical choice. By embracing the practicality, collaboration, and adaptability of CBT, individuals can begin a transformative journey toward effective anger management and improved well-being.

CONCLUSION

Managing anger with the help of CBT offers individuals a path toward profound personal growth and positive transformation. By embracing the principles and techniques of CBT, we equip ourselves with the necessary tools to navigate the complex landscape of our emotions and thoughts.

Through this process, we understand the relationship between our thoughts, emotions, and behaviors, empowering us to break free from anger and forge a more balanced and fulfilling life.

With the inclusion of CBT, we rewrite the narratives that fuel our anger, challenge distorted thoughts, and cultivate healthier responses to anger triggers. By doing so, we reclaim control over our emotions, enhancing our overall well-being and allowing us to thrive in our personal and interpersonal relationships choosing CBT as our pathway to anger management, we empower ourselves with a structured and evidence-based approach that addresses the underlying causes of our anger. It reduces stress levels, boosts self-confidence, and cultivates a deep sense of inner peace and satisfaction.

Choosing CBT for anger management is not just a short-term solution; it offers long-lasting and transformative benefits. By engaging in the process of self-reflection, introspection, and skill-building that CBT provides, we embark on a journey of self-discovery and personal growth. We develop a deeper understanding of ourselves, our triggers, and our patterns of thinking and behaving, allowing us to make conscious choices that lead to positive change.

As we conclude this chapter, I invite you to embrace the power of CBT in managing and transforming your anger. The journey requires commitment, patience, and self-compassion, but the rewards are immeasurable. By choosing CBT, you are choosing to take control of your emotions and reactions to break free from the cycle of anger and its negative consequences. Embrace this opportunity for growth and change and may CBT guide you toward a life of emotional well-being, healthier relationships, and a greater sense of inner peace.

YOUR FAREWELL
TO ANGER

As we conclude this book, let us reflect on the profound impact of controlling anger. It is a common experience to be overwhelmed by the intensity of the moment, succumbing to our emotions and reacting impulsively. However, we have uncovered an alternative approach. By exploring the insights and techniques presented in this book, we have discovered that anger is not an overwhelming force we cannot overcome. We have learned to identify triggers, recognize early signs of anger before it escalates, and respond in ways that are both constructive and beneficial to our well-being.

It's crucial to remember that anger is a natural human emotion and is not inherently wrong or bad. It's how we choose to react to anger that can cause problems. Uncontrolled anger can have harmful effects on ourselves and those around us, leading to feelings of frustration, regret, and pain. Therefore, it becomes imperative to address the underlying issues contributing to anger and develop effective coping mechanisms to manage it.

One of the most profound lessons we have learned is that anger is not a fixed state, but a dynamic process influenced by numerous factors—our thoughts, emotions, behaviors, external stress, relationships, and life events. By adopting a holistic approach and addressing all these factors, we gain a deeper understanding of our anger and develop more effective strategies for its management. We've learned that anger is neither a negative nor a shameful emotion but rather a natural and necessary part of being human. It arises in response to perceived threats, injustices, and boundary violations. Moreover, we have discovered how anger is expressed healthily and constructively without causing harm to ourselves or others.

The journey of controlling anger is not an easy path, and it will require patience, persistence, and a willingness to confront our limitations and vulnerabilities. However, the rewards are immeasurable. Taking control of anger grants us a greater sense of self-awareness, self-mastery, and self-respect. We forge stronger, more authentic relationships and navigate challenges with increased confidence and resilience. As we move forward, let us remember that the journey is continuous. Setbacks, challenges, and moments of frustration will arise, but our commitment to controlling anger empowers us to overcome these obstacles and continue to grow and evolve.

We must continue to practice mindfulness, self-compassion, and cognitive restructuring regularly. Seeking support from loved ones, therapists, or support groups is invaluable. Cultivating healthy habits, such as exercise, nutritious eating, and sufficient sleep, aids stress management and emotional regulation. Above all, maintaining a positive and growth-oriented mindset is crucial. Recognize that anger does not define us; it is a part of our experience that we can learn to manage and transform. Embrace the challenges of controlling anger as opportunities for growth and development, celebrating successes along the way.

If you continue struggling with anger, remember that you are not alone. Many individuals face similar challenges, and seeking help is a courageous act of strength, not weakness. You now possess valuable information to assemble a positive support team that can assist you on your journey. Therapy, support groups, and self-help techniques are adequate resources that can help manage anger and progress toward a more fulfilling life. This journey is ongoing, and armed with the right tools and knowledge, you can continue to make progress and lead a fulfilling life. Embrace the fact that you are not a finished product but rather a work in progress, evolving and growing throughout your entire life.

As we say farewell, let us hold on to the valuable lessons and insights we have gained, carrying them forward as we continue our journey toward greater self-awareness, self-mastery, and self-respect. Controlling anger is not a one-time destination; it is a lifelong journey of growth and personal development. Let us embrace this journey with passion, energy, and enthusiasm, knowing that with these qualities, we have the power to achieve anything we set our minds to. By cultivating a life filled with peace, joy, and fulfillment, we can create a positive impact not only on ourselves but also on the world around us. Farewell, and may your path be filled with success and happiness.

ABOUT THE AUTHOR

Greetings! I'm Ronald Normandy, and I am deeply passionate about exploring the human mind. While pursuing my bachelor's degrees in Psychology and Anatomy, my primary focus was studying the intricacies of the human mind and body. Driven by my thirst for knowledge, I have been fortunate to travel to several countries across the globe interacting with individuals from diverse racial, cultural, and socioeconomic backgrounds. Living abroad has allowed me to learn different languages and immerse myself in various cultures. These experiences have significantly influenced and shaped my unique perspective on life.

My personal experiences have given me an exceptional understanding of the challenges associated with anger management. This understanding has inspired me to offer my support to others who may be encountering similar issues. Over the years, I have been able to guide friends and family members, assisting them in navigating their relationships, overcoming personal struggles, and developing effective strategies to enhance their overall quality of life.

During my formative years, I encountered significant challenges with anger management, which profoundly impacted every aspect of my life. However, it was through counseling during my adolescence that I could undergo a transformative journey. I learned to replace negative patterns with constructive practices, such as engaging in sports and music. This process of self-discovery and personal growth has spanned over two decades, and I remain committed to continually deepening my understanding of myself and effectively managing my emotions.

While immersed in writing this book, I found it to be a profoundly therapeutic experience. Like many individuals, I have faced personal issues and struggles throughout my life. However, by assisting others in their own journeys, I am reminded that we all carry our own share of pain and trauma, even when it remains unacknowledged.

The goal of writing this book is to empower readers to effectively address their issues by providing them with the necessary tools and techniques. I aim to assist everyone in recognizing and reducing the negative emotions that have hindered progress. The knowledge and experiences I have accumulated over the years, both from my personal journey and from my educational endeavors, have firmly convinced me that it is possible to transform one's life, even when confronted with overwhelming anger and pain.

My aspiration is to contribute to normalizing discussions around topics often concealed and stigmatized. I hope to inspire readers to talk openly about their struggles and emotions, fostering an environment of understanding and support. By acknowledging and expressing our anger constructively, we can cultivate and maintain healthy and fulfilling lives, benefiting ourselves and those around us.

REFERENCES

Ackerman, C. E. (2017, March 20). *CBT techniques: 25 cognitive behavioral therapy worksheets.* Positive Psychology. https://positivepsychology.com/cbt-cognitivebehavioral-therapy-techniques-worksheets/

American Psychological Association. (2017, July 31). *Cognitive behavioral therapy (CBT).* https://www.apa.org/ptsd-guideline/treatments/cognitive-behavioraltherapy

Beydoun, M.A., & Wang, Y. (2010, June). *Pathways linking socioeconomic status to obesity through depression and lifestyle factors among young US adults.* PubMed. https://pubmed.ncbi.nlm.nih.gov/19853306/

Buddy, T. (2021, August 2). *The link between alcohol and aggression.* Verywell Mind. https://www.verywellmind.com/alcoholfacilitates-aggression-62647#:~:text=Alcohol%20impairs%20cogniti ve%20function%2C%20which,misread%20a%2 0situation%20and%20overreact.

CDC. (2022, June 2). *Death rate maps & graphs.* https://www.cdc.gov/drugoverdose/deaths/in dex.html

Durré, L. (n.d.). *10 signs of a positive work environment.* Monster. https://www.monster.com/careeradvice/article/10-signs-positive-workplace

Esquivel, M. K. (2022). Nutrition benefits and considerations for whole foods plant-based eating patterns. *American Journal of Lifestyle Medicine, 16*(3), 284–290. https://doi.org/10.1177/15598276221075992

Gasmi, A., Nasreen, A., Menzel, A., Gasmi Benahmed,

A., Pivina, L., Noor, S., Peana, M., Chirumbolo, S., & Bjørklund, G. (2022). Neurotransmitters regulation and food intake: The role of dietary sources in neurotransmission. *Molecules (Basel, Switzerland), 28*(1), 210. https://doi.org/10.3390/molecules28010210

Gokhool, N. (2022, April, 2). *Is your relationship making you anxious?* Women's Health. https://www.womenshealthmag.com/relations hips/a39489136/relationship-anxiety/

Goodreads. (n.d.) *Quote by Jim Rohn.* https://www.goodreads.com/quotes/1798you-are-the-average-of-the-five-people-youspend

Guh, D. P., Zhang, W., Bansback, N., Amarsi, Z., Birmingham, C. L., & Anis, A. H. (2009). The incidence of co-morbidities related to obesity and overweight: A systematic review and metaanalysis. *BMC public health, 9,* 88. https://doi.org/10.1186/1471-2458-9-88

Hall, W., & Degenhardt, L. (2008). Cannabis use and the risk of developing a psychotic disorder. *World Psychiatry: Official Journal of the World Psychiatric Association (WPA), 7*(2), 68–71. https://doi.org/10.1002/j.2051-5545.2008.tb00158.x

Harvard T. H. Chan School of Public Health. (n.d.). *Stress and health.* https://www.hsph.harvard.edu/nutritionsource /stress-and-health/

He, K., Hu, F. B., Colditz, G. A., Manson, J. E., Willett, W. C., & Liu, S. (2004). Changes in intake of fruits and vegetables in relation to risk of obesity and weight gain among middle-aged women. *International journal of obesity and related metabolic disorders: Journal of the International Association for the Study of Obesity, 28*(12), 1569–1574. https://doi.org/10.1038/sj.ijo.0802795

Holder, M. D. (2019, June 24). *The contribution of food consumption to well-being*. Karger. https://www.karger.com/Article/FullText/499 147

Hu, F. B. (2003). Plant-based foods and prevention of cardiovascular disease: an overview. *The American Journal of Clinical Nutrition, 78*(3 Suppl), 544S–551S. https://doi.org/10.1093/ajcn/78.3.544S

Jacka, F. N., Pasco, J. A., Mykletun, A., Williams, L. J., Hodge, A. M., O'Reilly, S. L., Nicholson, G. C., Kotowicz, M. A., & Berk, M. (2010).

Association of Western and traditional diets with depression and anxiety in women. *American Journal of Psychiatry, 167*(3), 305–311. https://doi.org/10.1176/appi.ajp.2009.0906088 1

Johnston, B. C., Kanters, S., Bandayrel, K., Wu, P., Naji, F., Siemieniuk, R. A., Ball, G. D., Busse, J. W., Thorlund, K., Guyatt, G., Jansen, J. P., & Mills, E. J. (2014). Comparison of weight loss among named diet programs in overweight and obese adults: a meta-analysis. *JAMA, 312*(9), 923–933. https://doi.org/10.1001/jama.2014.10397

Juul, F., Vaidean, G., & Parekh, N. (2021). Ultraprocessed Foods and cardiovascular diseases: Potential mechanisms of action. *Advances in nutrition (Bethesda, Md.), 12*(5), 1673–1680. https://doi.org/10.1093/advances/nmab049

Kaczkurkin, A. N., & Foa, E. B. (2105, September). *Cognitive-behavioral therapy for anxiety disorders: An update on the empirical evidence.* National Library of Medicines. https://www.ncbi.nlm.nih.gov/pmc/articles/P MC4610618/

Laitano, H. V., Ely, A., Sordi, A. O., Schuch, F. B., Pechansky, F., Hartmann, T., Hilgert, J. B., Wendland, E. M., Von Dimen, L., Scherer, J. N., Calixto, A. M., Narvaez, J. C. M., Ornell, F., & Kessler, F. H. P. (2022). Anger and substance abuse: A systematic review and meta-analysis. *Revista brasileira de psiquiatria (Sao Paulo, Brazil: 1999), 44*(1), 103–110. https://doi.org/10.1590/1516-4446-2020-1133

Lally, P., Van Jaarsveld, C. H. M., Potts, H. W. W., & Wardle, J. (2009). How are habits formed: Modeling habit formation in the real world. *European Journal of Social Psychology, 40*(6), 998– 1009. https://onlinelibrary.wiley.com/doi/abs/10.100 2/ejsp.674

Lazarus, C. N. (2010, August 13). *Mind over mood: Feeling better by thinking better.* Psychology Today. https://www.psychologytoday.com/us/blog/th ink-well/201008/mind-over-mood-feelingbetter-thinking-better

Managing anger: 8 tips to make it a positive experience. (n.d.). Live Your True Story. https://www.liveyourtruestory.com/managinganger-8-tips-to-make-it-a-positive-experiencecommunication/

Mann, T., Tomiyama, A. J., Westling, E., Lew, A. M., Samuels, B., & Chatman, J. (2007). Medicare's search for effective obesity treatments: Diets are not the answer. *The American Psychologist, 62*(3), 220–233. https://doi.org/10.1037/0003-066X.62.3.220

McIntyre, K. M., Mogle, J. A., Scodes, J. M., Pavlicova,
M., Shapiro, P. A., Gorenstein, E. E., Tager, F. A., Monk, C.,
Almeida, D. M., & Sloan, R. P. (2019). Anger-reduction treatment
reduces negative affect reactivity to daily stressors.

Journal of Consulting and Clinical Psychology, 87(2), 141–150.
https://doi.org/10.1037/ccp0000359

Mehri A. (2020). Trace elements in human nutrition (II)
- An update. *International Journal of Preventive
Medicine, 11*, 2.
https://doi.org/10.4103/ijpvm.IJPVM_48_19

Menjivar, J. (n.d.). *The dos and don'ts of friend drama*. Do Something.
https://www.dosomething.org/us/articles/thedos-and-donts-of-
friend-drama

Miguel, M. (2020, June 4). *The wise mind: How logical reasoning can help
manage emotions*. The University of Chicago: The Center for
Practical Wisdom.
https://wisdomcenter.uchicago.edu/news/discussions/wise-mind-
how-logical-reasoning-canhelp-manage-emotions

Morin, A. (2014, October 17). *5 scientific reasons you should choose your
friends carefully*. Forbes.
https://www.forbes.com/sites/amymorin/201 4/10/17/5-scientific-
reasons-you-shouldchoose-your-
friendscarefully/?sh=51b256816181

Nardocci, M., Polsky, J. Y., & Moubarac, J. C. (2021). Consumption of
ultra-processed foods is associated with obesity, diabetes and
hypertension in Canadian adults. *Canadian journal of public health =
Revue canadienne de sante publique, 112*(3), 421–429. |
https://doi.org/10.17269/s41997-020-00429-9

NIH. (2004, October). *Alcohol's damaging effects on the brain.* https://pubs.niaaa.nih.gov/publications/aa63/a a63.htm

NIH. (2015, November 18). *10 percent of US adults have drug use disorder at some point in their lives.* https://www.nih.gov/news-events/newsreleases/10-percent-us-adults-have-drug-usedisorder-some-point-their-lives

Oswald, R. (November 6, 2022). *7 anger management tips to prevent relationship damage.* Mayo Clinic. https://www.mayoclinichealthsystem.org/home town-health/speaking-of-health/7-angermanagement-tips-to-prevent-relationshipdamage

Peterson, T. J. & Troy, B. (2021, October 8). *Meditation for anger: How it works & tips for getting started.* Choosing Therapy. https://www.choosingtherapy.com/meditationfor-anger/

Pikiewicz. K. (2012, October 22). *Own anger to manage it.* Psychology Today. https://www.psychologytoday.com/us/blog/m eaningful-you/201210/own-anger-manage-it

Provencher, V., Drapeau, V., Tremblay, A., Després, J. P., & Lemieux, S. (2003). Eating behaviors and indexes of body composition in men and women from the Québec family study. *Obesity research, 11*(6), 783–792. |https://doi.org/10.1038/oby.2003.109

Quello, S. B., Brady, K. T., & Sonne, S. C. (2005). Mood disorders and substance use disorder: a complex comorbidity. *Science & practice perspectives, 3*(1), 13–21. https://doi.org/10.1151/spp053113

Rao, T. S., Asha, M. R., Ramesh, B. N., & Rao, K. S. (2008). Understanding nutrition, depression and mental illnesses. *Indian journal of psychiatry, 50*(2), 77–82. https://doi.org/10.4103/0019-5545.42391

Robinson, L. & Smith, M. (2020). *Social media and mental health*. Help Guide. https://www.helpguide.org/articles/mentalhealth/social-media-and-mentalhealth.htm#:~:text=However%2C%20multiple%20studies%20have%20found,about%20your%20life%20or%20appearance.

Scott, S. J. (2022, June 11). *19 strategies to let go of your anger and resentment*. Develop Good Habits. https://www.developgoodhabits.com/let-goanger/

Smith, K. (2022, November 18). *When anger becomes emotional abuse*. Psycom. https://www.psycom.net/control-angerfrustration-relationship

Stabler, C. M. (2021, September 1). *The effects of social media on mental health*. Lancaster General Health. https://www.lancastergeneralhealth.org/healthhub-home/2021/september/the-effects-ofsocial-media-on-mentalhealth#:~:text=The%20distraction%20can%20lead%20to,others%20enjoying%20a%20good%20time.

Staff, M.C. (2022, April 14). *Anger management: 10 tips to tame your anger*. Mayo Clinic Staff. https://www.mayoclinic.org/healthylifestyle/adult-health/in-depth/angermanagement/art-20045434

Te Morenga, L., Mallard, S., & Mann, J. (2012). Dietary sugars and body weight: systematic review and meta-analyses of randomised controlled trials and cohort studies. *BMJ (Clinical research ed.),* 346, e7492. https://doi.org/10.1136/bmj.e7492

Weiss, N. H., Goncharenko, S., Raudales, A. M., Schick, M. R., & Contractor, A. A. (2021). Alcohol to down-regulate negative and positive emotions: Extending our understanding of the functional role of alcohol in relation to posttraumatic stress disorder. *Addictive behaviors,*
115, 106777.
https://doi.org/10.1016/j.addbeh.2020.106777

Whiteman, H. (2017, February 10). *Eating more fruits, vegetables boosts psychological well-being in just 2 weeks.*
Medical News Today.
https://www.medicalnewstoday.com/articles/3
15781

World Health Organization. (2022, December 9). *WHO launches signature initiative to reduce cardiovascular disease through salt reduction and hypertension control.*
https://www.who.int/europe/newsroom/events/item/2022/12/09/de
faultcalendar/who-launches-signature-initiative-toreduce-
cardiovascular-disease-through-saltreduction

Younossi, Z. M., Koenig, A. B., Abdelatif, D., Fazel, Y., Henry, L., & Wymer, M. (2016). Global epidemiology of nonalcoholic fatty liver diseaseMeta-analytic assessment of prevalence, incidence, and outcomes. *Hepatology (Baltimore,*
Md.), 64(1), 73–84.
https://doi.org/10.1002/hep.28431

Yu, E., Malik, V. S., & Hu, F. B. (2018). Cardiovascular Disease Prevention by Diet Modification: JACC Health Promotion Series. *Journal of the American College of Cardiology, 72*(8), 914–926. https://doi.org/10.1016/j.jacc.2018.02.085

IMAGE REFERENCES

AbsolutVision. (2017, November 27). *Smileys* [Image]. Pixabay. https://pixabay.com/photos/smileyemoticon-anger-angry-2979107/

Altmann, G. (2017, August 29). *Choice* [Image]. Pixabay. https://pixabay.com/photos/choice-selectdecide-decision-vote-2692466/

Altmann, G. (2019, March 19). *Psychology* [Image]. Pixabay. https://pixabay.com/illustrations/brain-thinkthroughts-psychology-4065092/

Burden, A. (2016, February 13). *Pen* [Image]. Unsplash. https://unsplash.com/photos/y02jEX_B0O0

Crismariu, G. (2019, October 18). *Puzzled* [Image]. Unsplash. https://unsplash.com/photos/sOK9NjLArCw

Dumalo, N. (2018, March 27). *Optimism* [Image]. Unsplash. https://unsplash.com/photos/eZIzlTVgqNU

Duong, C. (2017, October 1). *Friendship* [Image]. Unsplash. https://unsplash.com/photos/Sj0iMtq_Z4w

Grabowska, K. (2015, May 31). *Puppet* [Image]. Pixabay. https://pixabay.com/photos/woodenmannequin-wooden-mannequin-791720/

Hain, J. (2014, November 26). *Brain* [Image]. Pixabay.
https://pixabay.com/illustrations/mind-brainmindset-perception-544404/

Hamiti, B. (2015, April 24). *Sunset* [Image]. Pixabay.
https://pixabay.com/photos/tree-sunsetclouds-sky-silhouette-736885/

Hartwan, ND. (2017, July 19). *Idea* [Image]. Pixabay.
https://pixabay.com/vectors/questions-manhead-success-lamp-2519654/

Hassan, M. (2018, June 6). *Mindset* [Image]. Pixabay.
https://pixabay.com/photos/mindset-brainstorming-tablet-woman-3455748/

Hernandez, K. (2020, April 17). *Rubik's cube* [Image].
Unsplash. https://unsplash.com/photos/LrlyZzX6Sws

Hunter, A. (2017, August 24). *Angry face* [Image].
Unsplash. https://unsplash.com/photos/5otlbgWJlLs

Kerckx, B. (2015, March 31). *Hearts* [Image]. Pixabay.
https://pixabay.com/photos/heart-loveromance-valentine-700141/

Koppens, Y. (2018, January 12). *Work desk* [Image]. Pixabay.
https://pixabay.com/photos/desksmartphone-iphone-notebook-3076954/

Koshkina, L. (2014, February 27). *Sunlight* [Image]. Pixabay.
https://pixabay.com/photos/flowersmeadow-sunlight-summer-276014/

Lacchmann-Anke, P.M. (2015, November 3). *Mental wall* [Image].
Pixabay.
https://pixabay.com/illustrations/drunk-wallill-stagger-bad-evil-1013898/

NL, R. (2020, April 12). *Sunset* [Image]. Pixabay. https://pixabay.com/photos/sunset-silhouettetwilight-5033708/

Pidvalnyi, O. (2021, November 26). *Balance* [Image]. Pixabay. https://pixabay.com/photos/balancedomino-business-risk-6815204/

Porter, R. (2021, January 24). *Driving* [Image]. Unsplash. https://unsplash.com/photos/phoEG7SinuM

Riva. E. (2017, February 13). *Mind* [Image]. Pixabay. https://pixabay.com/illustrations/brain-mindpsychology-idea-hearts-2062055/

Saidi, H. (2021, January 3). *Signboard* [Image]. Unsplash. https://unsplash.com/photos/9cgMKmZyhH0

Sierra, P. (2016, January 7). *Footprints* [Image]. Pixabay. https://pixabay.com/photos/sand-foot-printsprints-walking-1122958/

Sikkema, K. (2020, January 17). *Heart* [Image]. Unsplash. https://unsplash.com/photos/4le7k9XVYjE

Simmer, J. (2021, February 10). *Broken toy* [Image]. Unsplash. https://unsplash.com/photos/ZxRHtPacwUY

Sturgeon, C. (2018, September 11). Meditation [Image]. Unsplash. https://unsplash.com/photos/6KkYYqTEDw Q

Suhendra, W. (2020, March 19). *Unity* [Image]. Unsplash. https://unsplash.com/photos/Swk4G_xi_uM

Trochez, L. (2017, September 15). *Hope* [Image]. Unsplash. https://unsplash.com/photos/ktPKyUs3Qjs

Tulin, M. (2021, July 27). *Forgiveness* [Image]. Unsplash.
https://unsplash.com/photos/L7TkIKc0XnU

Turong, NN. (2020, Oct 8). *Women exercising.* [Image].

Pixabay. https://pixabay.com/illustrations/womenyoga-gym-healthy-exercise-5635784/

Wellington, J. (2015, June 1). *Garden harvest* [Image].
Pixabay.
https://pixabay.com/photos/vegetablesgarden-harvest-organic-790022/

Printed in Great Britain
by Amazon

41613878R00121